D0772379

You're Not

Who You Think You Are

A Blueprint for Retrieving Your Authentic Self

You're Not
Who You Think You Are

A Blueprint for Retrieving
Your Authentic Self

Albert Clayton Gaulden

Foreword by James Redfield

The Sedona Intensive Press

All names have been fictionalized to maintain client confidentiality and anonymity. Timelines have been compressed. Portions of this book appeared in *Clearing for the Millennium*.

Copyright © 2006 by Albert Clayton Gaulden
All rights reserved.

The Sedona Intensive Press
Post Office Box 2309
Sedona, Arizona 86339-2309

Printed in the United States of America
First Printing: September 2006

Library of Congress Control Number: 2006935537

Library of Congress Cataloging-in-Publication Data

Gaulden, Albert Clayton.
    You're not who you think you are / Albert Clayton Gaulden.
        p. cm.
    ISBN 0-615-13159-X
    1. Gaulden, Albert Clayton. 2. Astrologers—United States—Biography. 3. Spiritual life. I. Title.

Book design and composition by Steve Hansen

Special Appreciation for Scott Carney

This book would never have been started, much less finished and published, had it not been for the persistent nagging, cajoling, pushing, and encouragement from my business partner, Scott Carney. I consider this book as much his as it is mine—he is truly the co-author in every way. Scott helped shape this book by rewriting a lot of the material, editing and refining words, taking out and adding ideas, and making the flow of the manuscript smoother and more readable. He had very pointed and oftentimes different opinions than mine. But there is more to this acknowledgment than just *You're Not Who You Think You Are.*

Scott Carney has developed into a true business partner. He is diligent in keeping us organized and committed to helping change the lives of those who sign on for our personal growth program. Scott has studied astrology vigorously and fine-tuned his innate intuition to become his own brand of effective practitioner.

Thanks to Scott for helping me to be a better person and for helping me to publish *You're Not Who You Think You Are* as a guidebook for how to be authentically connected to a power greater than oneself.

Dedication

To the Bells, David, Gail, Ashley and Andrew

and

Susan Sarandon

Contents

Warning

This is a dangerous book.

Warning

It has challenging lessons and hidden messages.

Warning

When you scan the pages, you will understand.

Warning

The eyes have it.

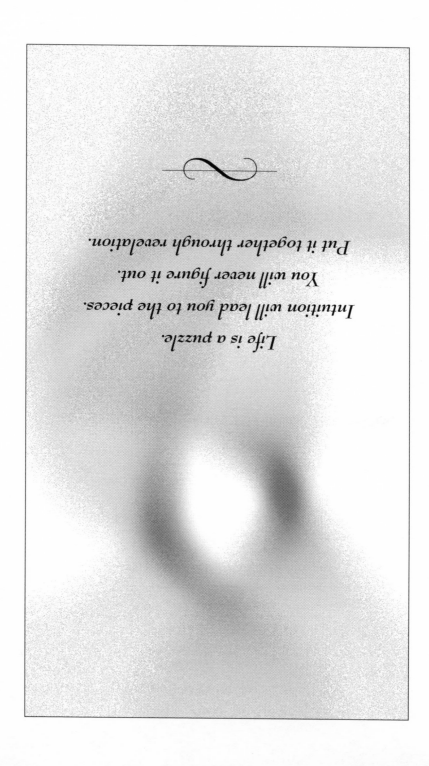

Life is a puzzle.
Intuition will lead you to the pieces.
You will never figure it out.
Put it together through revelation.

Foreword

by James Redfield,
author of *The Celestine Prophecy*

I first heard of Albert Gaulden from a friend who went to see him on one of his many work trips to Alabama. "He is unbelievably accurate in bringing personality issues to the surface," she told me over coffee one day. "He really nailed the way I was getting in my own way, blocking my potential. You can't hide anything from Albert."

After several other people synchronistically mentioned this astro-intuitive and therapist, I found myself thoroughly intrigued, so I called his booking agent and got in line, finally meeting Albert several days later in the Pickwick Hotel in Birmingham. It took only a few minutes for Albert's transparent personality to shine through. He is witty, mildly sarcastic, and an absolutely hilarious storyteller. And he is totally serious about what he does with his clients.

Quickly disposing of the initial banter, he beckoned me to a corner couch and placed a completed astrological chart on the table between us.

"Well," he remarked, "you're quite a secretive fellow, aren't you … and in a lot of conflict?" He went on to tell me that at this time in my life, the planet Pluto was exactly 90 degrees from where it was the day I was born. This is an occurrence that signals a period in which everything in a person's life that is not conducive to his higher learning and psychological growth tends to blow up and be taken away, sometimes traumatically.

I smiled at him, remaining aloof, but he was, in fact, right on target. My life was undergoing a vast reorganization. I had ended a marriage and left a job I had held for eight years.

"Ah, yes," he continued, "there's more. You're also writing something. What is it?"

"Wait a minute," I interrupted. "How did you know that?"

He pushed the chart around where I could see it. "It's right here. You've got Venus and Jupiter in Aquarius in the fifth house being activated by transit and progression."

Now I was impressed. I had started writing *The Celestine Prophecy* about six months earlier. "I want to understand how you do this," I said.

Albert laughed, and the ensuing conversation led to a trip to Sedona to go through his famous Sedona Intensive, where Albert performed his amazing gift: helping to pull into consciousness those unconscious habits and addictions that keep us from a greater life. In my case, of course, we focused on my aloofness and reluctance to commit to a single project. With the help of Sedona herself (those magic red hills alone seem to increase the synchronicity and provide the experiences that illustrate whatever we are learning), I became aware of exactly when my indifference kicks in, why it gets in the way, and what my real self feels like when I break free of this control drama.

In this environment, I was able to spend the dedicated free time to survey my life as one story—from that first placement with my early family all the way through the twists and turns of my subsequent experience. I found hidden meaning in old relationships, misdeeds that needed rectifying, and full acknowledgment of the preparation my past seemed to have provided me. Most of all I was to connect with a sense of freedom and inspiration that comes from living one's life honestly, with as few secrets as possible.

In retrospect, I think that Albert's emphasis on addictions and unconscious habits brought home for me the wisdom of such thinkers as Norman O. Brown and Ernest Becker, who years ago explained that we humans can evolve no further until we learn to deal with our everyday compulsions—those parts of our individual lifestyles we pursue with singular intensity, and at which we resist looking because they seem to feel so good. We know now that such activities, which can be of varying degrees of destructiveness—overworking, eating, playing, TVing, shopping, judging, distancing, complaining, drinking, drugging—are all unconsciously designed to keep us distracted, and to fend off the ego's fear of facing the great mystery that is this life. The ego fights this recognition because it senses that it must lose total control, and because it has no idea that such recognition would merely mean expanding into a higher self full of intuition and creativity and grand adventure.

In his book, Albert seeks to convey the full scope of such a clearing and opening process. In his humorous and—yes—confrontational way, he has clearly laid out the challenge facing all of us. We can talk about a coming spiritual renaissance to any degree we want, but it cannot happen until enough of us grasp that spiritual growth has a mental health component. We all have to step back and really look at the parts of our personalities that hold us back, because only then can we become who we really are—and truly move forward into a consciousness and mission that changes the world.

Book I

Retrieving Albert

Chapter 1

Reconnecting to the High Self

The first time I met Swami Swahananda, the spiritual head of the Vedanta Society in Southern California, I had been hired by a close friend who was a Vedantist to meet with this venerated spiritual leader to discuss his astrological birth chart. He was very interested in what I had to say and later told me that my information was very accurate. In a conversation of general discussion following his reading, I declared that I didn't believe in gurus and I would never join a cult. He said it was better for me to believe in myself. I learned from him that guru means teacher in Sanskrit and Vedanta is not a cult. A lot of us have contempt before we investigate a person or an "ism" which is how ignorance and misinformation choke an open-minded attitude to death.

Later when I was facing an important decision, I intuitively knew that he was the one who could help me. After discussing my problem, Swami gave me a book, *How to Know God* which instructs the novice to the teachings of Vedanta on how to become one with the Divine within. A few months later I told Swami that I wanted to become a Vedantist. He became my teacher. (I learned the hard way never to say "never".)

"When you did my chart several months ago, you quoted Shakespeare: 'All the world's a stage, and all the men and women merely players ....' If you will take the role of my astrologer in the play you wrote (called life), then I will take the part of the guru," he said with a chuckle.

At my initiation, he gave me a Sanskrit name, Ramapriya, which means beloved of God, not to conceal my identity within an alias but to celebrate my spiritual rebirth. Only he, nuns from the Sarada Convent, and other devotees call me by that name.

Many sects and spiritual leaders use control tactics to make followers dependent on them. It is dangerous and manipulative for an organization or leader to control another person's life, telling him how to pray and what to believe, and taking away his freedom to make mistakes along the way.

"Who am I?"

My guru sat across from me. I had booked a sitting in his spartan rooms at the Vedanta Center in Hollywood.

"To know God is to know you," Swami said.

God had been a fly in the ointment when I got sober. This aphorism, "to know God is to know you," started me exploring deep-tissue issues I had around God. It turned out to be a resentment against church leadership, and not a disdain for God, that was the problem.

Swami listened as I complained about my career as an astro-intuitive. Clients ask incessantly, "Where is the money?" Will I have a new lover in my future?" "Why do bad things keep happening?" I had no more answers. I had questions for Swami.

Astrology had been my career before I got sober, but predicting the future never interested me. I book appointments with clients hour after hour. Some hear what I have to say and go out and create a better life. Others do the same self-destructive things with the same ruinous results.

Are clients able to have a better life because I say so? Only God knows. I never take credit for their good fortune, and I don't take the blame when things don't work out. Some charts show success while others are mediocre. A lot of people are psychic leeches desperate for someone to make their lives better without seeing the cause and effect within them.

My motive for speaking to Swami was to end my career as an astro-intuitive and instead sell books in the Vedanta library or to be Swami's personal assistant. I was burned out as a stargazer and I felt as if I were dying.

"Ramapriya, when you first came to me you were full of compassion for the suffering alcoholic, were you not?"

"Yes."

"You told me then that you had to share with others what had been given to you, did you not?"

"That is true, Swami."

"When you had been sober for a few years, you wanted to move to Hawaii with a rich lady. She wanted a companion, and you wanted to oblige. I said God wanted you to continue your work; the sun could wait."

Before Swami reminded me what I wanted the year after that, he ordered Darjeeling tea and handed me prasad, food consecrated on the altar in the temple.

"A year later you came to counsel with me and you told me you hated Sedona. You said people there were spiritually shallow. You wanted to move to the monastery in Montecito, California. I said that if you didn't like Sedona, you wouldn't like Montecito. You stayed in Sedona."

Swami is an old man with the razor-sharp memory of a much younger man, I mused to myself.

"In India," Swami said, "there is a Sufi story about creation and where to put God. 'If we put God at the bottom of the ocean, man will dive there. Place God on the mountaintop, man will climb there. But if we put God inside him, man will never think to look there.'"

Sometimes I have trouble knowing when natural law is operating in my life. Swami was leading me where I didn't want to go. I always resist, and then the God I cannot see takes over and my life gets better.

"Ramapriya, permit the clients to come to you for counsel, especially when they seem attached to illusion. See God in each one of them long enough, and one day God will reach out and touch you."

"But Swami, there must be more to my life than one-hour sessions with curiosity seekers who think I can magically make their lives better."

As is his character, Swami sat silently with his eyes closed for several minutes. I always suspect that he moves quickly into samadhi, a deathlike sleep, when he meditates.

"Go home and light a fire under people. Help students find out who they are. Tell them that God remembers what they forgot," Swami said.

He and I had a silent luncheon alone. After we ate we went to the temple and he chanted while I remained quiet. Swami walked me to my car, and as I got in to leave, he tapped on my window.

"Ramapriya, you said to me today that you thought you were dying. You are dying. You are dying to the un-you to become authentic. Stop trying to control everything. God will lead the way. When He is ready for your life to change, your path will bend and you will go there. Your life is not your concern. Fear not. God is building your road as we speak."

Within days of my return home, a metaphysical bookstore in my hometown called to ask me to speak at a conference. I accepted the invitation. The God I could not see and could not touch had set the wheels of karma in motion for the next leg of my spiritual journey.

Returning to Birmingham reminded me of my alcoholic past—years of boozing and bamboozling. In the days of double martinis, I lost all hope in a mud slide of compulsive drinking. And I moved a lot. Now the prophet without honor was going home and getting paid for it.

I was going back as an astro-intuitive and counselor, mixing the principles of astrology with Jungian psychology and my sixth sense. I am also adept at deciphering voice imprint. As the client speaks, I get thought impressions from the resonance of his voice. Helping heal character defects that show up in the astrological horoscopes of clients is my brand of therapy. I travel to major cities throughout the world to give seminars and consult with clients, from actors to professional athletes to Wall Street moguls to people in all sorts of professions.

The crowd seemed to enjoy my lecture. I signed up ten people for a trip to Egypt's sacred sites that I would be hosting six months later. After an early dinner with friends, I returned to the hotel, packed, and decided to rest before catching the red-eye to Southern California.

I slipped my favorite CD into the entertainment console as I lay on the bed to reflect on the day's activities. In a matter of minutes I nodded off. And then, as if guided by a breath coach, I began to breathe as I do when I am meditating: a repetition of deep, slow breaths, in through the nose and out through the mouth. Soon my inhales and exhales became deeper and more rhythmic. My body felt weightless.

Oddly, within a few minutes my lips began to tingle and I struggled to catch my breath. I had the impression that someone was trying to speak through me. My palms were sweaty. I felt hot, then ice-cold. At first I seemed to free-fall, but fear caused me to wake up, which silenced whoever wanted to speak. I closed my eyes again and took several relaxing breaths. I let go completely and spiraled into darkness where there were intermittent flashes of bright light.

I focused on a white pyramid. A pyramid first appeared in my daydreams when I was a boy. A powerful and resonant male voice spoke.

Albert, why did it take you so long to talk with me?

"Oh, my God, who is this?" I lashed out.

I was startled awake and sat up on the edge of the bed. Where was this voice coming from? I paced the room drinking large gulps of mineral water. For years I had heard that some of my friends communicated with dead people. I wanted nothing to do with an entity from the spirit world if that's what this man was.

However, energy pulled me back to the bed. I lay down and slipped back into meditation.

Relax. Continue to breathe evenly and you will gradually let go of fear. I have been monitoring you. Your actions and thoughts indicate that you are ready to communicate with me mind to mind.

The clearest explanation I can give of this energy connection is that the communication was intuitive. I did not and still do not have out-loud conversations with this invisible guide. The odd thing was that instinctively I have always known there was a part of me that had never exposed itself. Although I would ask a million questions to validate him, this being has kept me alive and sane throughout my life. Through the years I have counseled a lot of clients who swear they have connected with someone "inside" they could not talk about for fear of being labeled crazy.

I was not afraid, but I wanted proof of who had me under his spell. I instinctively knew he was scanning my intelligence. These thought impressions came to me with ease and authority.

I have been trying to talk to you for more than ten years.

"Why?" I asked.

You teach students that God is within. I am here to remind you that you're someone other than who you think you are. I am the microcosmic God. I am Paul, your High Self guide and teacher. When you reach the deepest level of consciousness I am that part of you who speaks. I am here to help you see things more clearly, as well as to confirm what you know and what more you have to remember.

If truth be told, all my life, at some level, I had been anticipating a connection—a validation of everything I knew to be true for me. To be able to exchange ideas with and ask questions of a source like Paul made life-long struggles with my identity worth every minute of the pain of separation and alienation from everybody in my life. To know that Paul was me and I was him satisfied my need not to give my power away and not to be controlled by any person or group, particularly by church dogma.

"Initially you tried to speak through me. I don't want anyone invading me against my free will," I said.

Because you were at such a deep level of consciousness, it seemed as if I were trying to talk through you. I am a part of you and will communicate only to you. You will decide what information you share with others.

"Are you an alien? Have you come to abduct me?" I asked.

Albert, I am not foreign to you and I have not come to take you away. I am the all-seeing, all-knowing part of you connected to the continuum of time. You and I are like spiritual twins.

Aha! Both in humor and dead seriously I have said that there were two Alberts. As Paul spoke to me, I did a gut check to see if I agreed with him. On all accounts, what he said rang true.

"Do you intend to dominate me with mind control?"

No. You have a mind of your own, which is controlled by what people think of you and what you must do to be accepted by others. You need to learn to be your own authority.

It took me awhile to check Paul out and to trust myself in trusting him. I don't cotton to hocus-pocus. A metaphysical troublemaker is how a lot of people describe me.

Because so many people die unaware, they don't know about soul growth on the other side. The dead hang around the Earth and interfere with the living. I liken it to a houseguest who won't go home. Paul definitely was not the undead.

A woman I know and admire, noted psychologist Dr. Edith Fiore, wrote a book called *The Unquiet Dead* about how dead people, or as she refers to them, displaced persons, inhabit the bodies and minds of those still living. Dr. Fiore asserts that possession is the root cause of depression, phobias, and addictions, conditions that she feels no amount of orthodox treatment can cure.

Through years of studying Eastern religions and paranormal psychology, I learned to trust my gut instinct. Because Paul identified himself as the God part of me, I let him tell me what this contact was about.

He explained that all of us have a quantum-physics reservoir of past lives to tap into. Paul said I am neither special nor privileged. Every person has his own High Self guide who can help him detach from what others believe or say.

Each of us is divided into three selves: a low self, a middle self, and a High Self. The low self is ego, which is pleasure bound. The middle self is mediator, which is truth bound. The High Self is God, who is the Great Redeemer.

Paul advised that one must be clear to hear the voice of inspiration. I wasn't certain what clearing meant, but he told me that we must get rid of the chaos that stifles the still, small voice of intuition.

There are channelers who purport to communicate with entities. J. Z. Knight, a medium who recently appeared in the film *What the Bleep Do We Know?*, claims that a five-million-year-old being whom she calls Ramtha speaks through her. Paul is not such a being. I am uncertain about channeling. But just because I think channelers are a questionable lot doesn't mean this stuff is not coming from somewhere. Evidently it's coming from one's High Self.

Dead talkers bug me. Something about invoking spirit contact doesn't click with me. Believing that dead people can talk through a medium is suspect. However, some people seem to be helped by them. I suggest you approach such communication with healthy skepticism.

When I asked Paul why he only spoke to me in meditation, he said that I am too scattered to listen to guidance. Meditation, he continued, is where the mind is still and the will is receptive. The clearer I became, he advised, the more easily I would be able to counsel without conscious contact with him. He and I would be as one.

I would speak as Albert, but the source of the information would be Paul, my High Self. All of this rang true to me, even though I often feel my mind is like a free-range chicken, furtive and restless. Paul suggested I change my ways if I wanted to be able to let High Self guide me.

One question addressed a trust issue. "If you are an aspect of me and not a separate entity, why do you call yourself Paul?"

Assigning a name distinguishes who is speaking. You need to know when it is your ego influencing you or your High Self that is talking.

It was you who intuited my name in awareness classes at the Spiritualist church in Los Angeles in the '70s. Your teacher taught you how to contact your inner guide. You silently called the name you assigned me, Paul. Your arms felt a shiver chill, or goose bumps, to confirm that I was present. Until this time you were never able to get out from under the influence of your ego long enough to hear me.

Anyone who wants to contact his High Self can. Advise students to sit quietly each day at a set time and call a name intuitively, as you did with me. Making an appointment at the same time each day increases the possibility of contact with one's soul whisperer.

Today you were afraid of me because I called your name. You never trusted that I would be able to communicate with you. You have lived in fear and distrust. I broke through the defense lines of your ego. Before, I intuitively influenced you without your conscious awareness.

Paul said that he is the God within me. God is within each of us. The reason that he is revealing himself to me is because the world as we know it is ending. The world that egocentric man made is going to pass away. There is a rebirth taking place moment to moment. It is the responsibility of each of us to experience the death of the false self.

Paul confirmed his presence throughout my life by recalling crises I had endured. When I was six years old, I fell twenty feet onto a gravel yard. My face was cut and scabbed and I was unconscious for several minutes, but there were no broken bones.

I took that fall with you. And—remember the car wreck in 1962?

Driving home to Alabama from Charleston Air Force Base in my brand new white MGB convertible, I fell asleep at the wheel and woke up just in time to swerve right into a ravine. The car hit nose-first, and I was thrown free of the top-down convertible into deep layers of freshly mown hay. I suffered a mild concussion, but again, no broken bones.

I nudged you before you hit the sixteen-wheeler truck head-on, guiding you to turn right onto a soft landing.

"How were you able to save my life when others die prematurely?" I asked.

Karma. It was not your time to die. Each of you chooses when to be born and when to die.

The soul knows there is no death. The true self knows that the perfect place, the Upper World, is real. Life on Earth is an illusion. The regret one feels when he dies is that he never knew his authentic self and he did not understand the mysteries of life that are all around him.

Death is like going from one room to another. The hell that scared you as a boy is hell on Earth and not in a dark, fiery place of condemnation for your sins or your disbelief in Jesus.

The Upper World is perfect-world consciousness, and the Lower World is chaotic. One needs to crack codes of unsolved mysteries to discover his authentic self, so as not to become attached to Earth-bound illusion.

The reason ancient schools of spiritual teachings used puzzles and riddles and had various levels of initiation was to make it harder for the ego to dominate man. The ego uses pleasures to entrap. God uses the spirit of the soul to free.

"How will I solve mysteries?" I asked.

Follow your stars.

Paul was confirming what I have been teaching for a long time. Kabbalah and I agree that everything you need to know and everywhere you need to go is in your birth chart.

"Paul, why don't I do what I am supposed to do?"

You are attached to material illusion and false perceptions. The calendar you consult is a timepiece of materialism. When you still your mind, you and I can communicate about who you are and what you need to do.

When you drank alcoholically, I urged you to take the tougher road back to God. Alcoholism was a great opportunity to clear away what separated you from God. The ego suggested you switch from hard liquor to wine, or that you needed a vacation. The ego never mentioned the name of God. God and forgiveness are anathema to the ego.

I was transfixed as Paul went on to describe the origin of the Earth and mankind. Lucifer got in a power struggle with God. Angel souls left God and the Upper World—thus the Lower World, although controlled by the ego, was established as a school for remembering life's lessons, prerequisites for return to the Upper World. Every deed and thought in contradiction to spiritual laws of the Upper World must be atoned for here on Earth. That part of me, spellbound by the ego, must free itself of the ego's false promises. I cannot access that knowledge of truth, love, beauty, and light as Albert, but I can as High Self. When I meditate I can connect to the one-true-God-created soul I always was.

Every soul has a resonance with God. The divine frequency is reactivated initially by flashes of intuition of harmony and peace. But the magnetism of the ego is strong; man is drawn back to the pleasure chest. But God is still alive within every soul.

Paul also told me:

A longing to return home pulls you like metal to a magnet when you choose to listen to High Self. Souls for centuries have anticipated an activation of the vibration of universal consciousness that shall support all who choose God and a reunion with original Oneness. You have a choice.

I did not understand this at first, but I later discovered that each of us has been in a Rip Van Winkle–like sleep state but significantly connected to an eternal resonance with God. The conscious mind does not know how to respond to this resonance because of its attachment to the ego. But a time will come when this resonance will dispel the influences of the ego.

Next, Paul said:

All of you on Earth work off karma from past lives by being in service to others. When a life ends, to have loved and to have served are the only attributes that matter.

The cosmic geometry aligns to support all who seek to go back to God. Watch the heavens and celestial movement. When Venus crosses the Sun in 2012, time as you know it will draw to a close. Configurations and signs of providential change are written in the sky maps.

It became time for you to make a choice to clear away blocks and barriers to your true identity, as you have satisfied conditions of karma from the seventy past lives that created it. All human beings live life after life after life.

I did not question Paul further about past lives. I knew intuitively that we have lived thousands of lives, in different galaxies and dimensions.

"What exactly is the assignment?" I asked.

Your assignment is to break away from the ego's control by clearing past-life and present karma; to make amends for harm that you have done to others; to live better than you speak and to live justly, love mercy, and walk humbly with God. Past deeds have separated you from God and made you a slave to your ego. You have agreed to clear others with the lessons you find along your path. You have hidden your true identity to protect yourself. You're not who you think you are. And nothing is what it seems. You are of the light.

"Am I the only one to lead others to the light?"

No, Albert, you are not. Liken this to a roundup of souls who want to return home. I have made contact with you as others are becoming reconnected to their High Selves. You were eventually able to hear my contact and to respond. Others will hear their guidance.

"What is the message?" I queried.

The end of the world of illusion is at hand. The world as it truly is will be made manifest. You must uncover your true self and help others to find their true selves. You are interrelated and interconnected. You will know one another by sound and by light.

I was riveted. Stone-still, I listened, and my heart raced.

There will be a homecoming of prodigals. Souls will come back spiritually balanced, having spent lifetimes looking for the other part of themselves in someone else.

For those who choose to clear, chaos will end. The conflicts that rage within will cease. Millions of souls are beginning to anticipate this event. The Lower World will be as the Upper World. It is said, "as above, so below."

"End times ..." I whispered through parched lips.

No, it is the beginning of time. Ancient prophecies will give you a deeper understanding of the period of endings and new beginnings.

Dr. Jose Arguelles became well known during the Harmonic Convergence in August 1987, when he wrote *The Mayan Factor* about the evolution of consciousness. Arguelles mentioned that 2012 would be the end of the Mayan calendar. Many people believed that he was predicting the end of the world.

Your message is to clear away the wreckage of your past and help others remember where they come from, as you will remember your own true ancestry.

"Are we all fallen angels? Are we all at the same level of soul growth?" I asked.

All of you are fallen angels, even those of you who act otherwise. Every soul on Earth must experience death and resurrection to be able to return to the Upper World.

You are at various stages of spiritual development. You were created equal in the beginning. The fall from grace changed the frequency. Lost souls disconnected from the Source. Life after life you make progress or backslide in your attempt to get home.

Millions of people will rediscover their true selves as their resonance with peace, truth, love, and light grows stronger.

"Paul, what are we trying to clear?" I asked.

In the beginning of Earth time your false self turned towards the dark side, away from God. That false self needs to die in order to leave darkness behind and rekindle the light within you.

"How?" I asked.

You must admit how egocentric concepts, self-centered ideas, hurtful deeds, harsh words, and parasitic mind perversions have kept you in darkness, separated from God, behaving contrary to your true self. Imperative for return to the rekindled light within is purification; a cleansing which requires dispensing with false disguises and bogus identification to reveal who you truly are: a precious child of God.

To clear means to repudiate thoughts and deeds committed by adhering to persuasions of the ego. This cannot be accomplished with occasional meditation and sporadic prayer or spiritual revival or momentary relief through song or seminar. Man is sick at a deep soul level.

In these times leading up to 2012, an inter-dimensional door will open. There will be a consciousness jolt and shift. Man will wake up to God-self and want to go home—balanced. But the price is to clear what has caused the separation from the Creator.

One final answer to your question of what you are trying to clear: As a surgeon would probe a patient to remove every cell of cancer, or a composer would fine-tune his concerto so there is not one false note in its resonance, mankind must clean up its karmic misdeeds that stand between him and God. It is time to return home.

Chapter 2

Mysteries and the Mayan Calendar

Paul had thrown floodlights on my dark side. Many times I had tried to bribe God into looking at some of the good in my life as a way to deflect attention from the scoundrel I had been. I have often referred to myself as a Jekyll-and-Hyde living in a demimonde. I can shift from loving to mean in a nanosecond. Many times I have asked myself, "Where is this nasty side coming from?" Evidently it is living in a storehouse of unholy thoughts and deeds that have festered. Since I had done little to clean up these dark parts of me, they had gotten so out of hand that a duplicitous dichotomy had been born in the underbelly of my consciousness.

I don't believe in Armageddon. The world will not go up in smoke because of man's sins. But what was this coming spiritual revolution all about? Could it be that war in the Middle East will escalate beyond human comprehension? Would there be some divine intervention to end the war? Did this have to do with global warming? My mind was jabbering like a gaggle of geese. A countdown had begun, and I wanted to run.

Computer technology may be the Antichrist, because it sucks so many of us into pornography, gambling, and on-line trading. Young people obsess over chat rooms and games like GMud and

EVE, which feed their dark side. On the other hand, cyberspace is the fastest way to get information.

I turned on my laptop and searched for anything I could find about what lies ahead of us. I entered Mayan calendar, end times, earth changes, global warming, and 2012 into a search engine. If my intuition could conjure this stuff up, there had to be confirmation or negation somewhere.

As a small boy, I was passionate about books. Years later, working in a law firm, I spent hours in the stacks of the Birmingham Public Library, whiling away my lunch hour exploring out-of-date books and reading personal papers and diaries of well-known public figures. The library was a sanctuary from my stressful yet bland childhood. I hopped on the bus most weekends to escape to a world of make-believe.

The intuition of my youth took me to certain areas in the library where I discovered documents like *The Secret Teachings of All Ages* by Manley P. Hall. Manley Hall looked like silent-screen actor John Barrymore and had the credentials of a college professor. In the preface to his book, Hall said that he was an intimate of the crown prince of Sweden. As a twelve-year-old boy, I was duly impressed by Manley Hall.

The Secret Teachings of All Ages covered everything in the occult, from alchemy to sorcery and black magic, even Kabbalah—and many other schools of thought I'd never heard discussed in the Baptist church. The dictionary revealed that the word occult simply means hidden.

Now, here online was a treasure trove of books that could give me some answers, just a click away. I found information on global warming. The National Academy of Sciences reported that the "recent warmth is unprecedented for at least the last 400 years and potentially for the last several millennia." Air pollution is diminishing our protective ozone layer, affecting weather patterns.

Northcentral University in Prescott, Arizona offered statistical proof that the planet is heating up. Ten of the past fourteen years were the hottest in history. In Sedona, winter weather is ten to twelve degrees warmer than it was when I moved here twenty-five years ago, and summer temperatures have risen five to six degrees in the same period of time. Glaciers are retreating, lakes are shrinking, and the polar ice caps are getting smaller by the day. Hurricanes, cyclones, and tornadoes are expected to increase in velocity and frequency due to rising temperatures, and destruction to property and people could be more catastrophic than anything the earth has endured thus far.

Former Vice President Al Gore reset the course of his life to focus on a last-ditch, all-out effort to help save the planet from irrevocable change. He narrated *An Inconvenient Truth,* a compelling film which points out that history is sitting on a ticking time bomb.

If the world's scientists are right, this eye-opening film points out, we have just ten years to avert a major catastrophe that could send our entire planet into a tailspin of destruction involving weather, floods, epidemics, and killer heat waves unlike anything we have ever experienced. Thankfully, in addition to its gory scientific data, the film offered steps we as human beings can take to alter the course of devastation that awaits us if we don't change how we deplete resources and emit carbon dioxide into the atmosphere.

What can you do to join the clean-up detail? How can you be a part of the global warming turnaround? Begin at home. Start to recycle. Conserve electricity by switching to energy-efficient light bulbs and rethinking how you use power in your house. Investigate solar energy for your home or office. Carpool. Ride a bicycle. I am considering buying a hybrid automobile.

Emmy Award-winning author of the best selling book, *The Case Against Lawyers,* Court TV anchor Catherine Crier weighs in on temperatures rising when she said that "just a sea rise of a meter or so around the world will not only reshape Florida and Manhattan, but displace hundreds of millions of people from Shanghai to Haiti. In 2003 the European heat wave claimed forty-nine thousand lives in eight countries alone."

Crier goes on to say that "already rising temperatures have decreased grain output by ten percent—in 2003 it was down 17% right here in the United States. When the thermometer rises, plants reduce photosynthesis, prevent pollination and become dehydrated, thus decreasing yields. And where are you going to get fresh water? As the temperature goes up, the mountain snow and ice reservoirs are melting, rivers are drying up at home and around the world, and the below ground water tables are dropping. Forget wars over oil … watch out for the fights over fresh water."

Crier recommends that "whether you agree with the notion of global warming, get educated. Here's a book you can download for free. It's called *Plan B 2.0: Rescuing a Planet under Stress and a Civilization in Trouble* by Lester Brown. Log on to **www.earthpolicy.org** or you can donate to the cause by actually buying the book."

Global warming is a fact of life. We can take our planet back by taking better care of her. Do not wait for someone else; do your part now. You and I created global warming, so you and I can un-create it. The ozone layer can be replenished if we start today. Wait a few years, and it will be too late.

Next, I turned my inquiry to the Mayan calendar. Having scanned a few sources, I felt that some of the texts were too complicated or smacked of hearsay. I often find that metaphysical seekers take an idea and build a case without sufficient investigation. It is important for me to understand a point of view and feel confident of its legitimacy. The telltale way that I legitimize documents or books or ideas is to rely on my intuition. If something doesn't ring true for me, I leave it where I found it. I always ask myself, 'Are these actual revelations or speculative conjectures?'

Distinguishing between fact and fiction regarding the Mayan material was a daunting task that required careful discernment to get to the bottom of the mystery. Was the calendar a sign of endings or of new beginnings? I was determined to stay the course until I knew for myself which it was.

Not your run-of-the-mill calendar, the Tzolkin, as it is called, originated in at least the 6th century BCE. It is reputed to be the most accurate datebook in the world, due in part to its relative complexity; it uses cycles of 13 and 20, relating to the movement of Venus and other planets, and it incorporates twenty-two different subcalendars.

The Mayans approached prophecy by deeply studying the periodicity of cycles, especially astronomical ones, and their connection to human events. For the layman, astrology is an interpretation of what it means when planets are in certain configurations, forming geometric alignments with one another and especially at critical times like solar and lunar eclipses and at the equinoxes. We astrologers call astrology the art of interpreting astronomy.

Looming large are 32 solar and lunar eclipses between September 2006 and November 28, 2012 and the transit of Pluto through the sign of Capricorn. (See the list on page 246.)

A solar eclipse occurs when the Moon passes in front of the Sun, partially or completely blocking its light. A lunar eclipse is when the Earth passes directly in front of the Moon, casting its shadow on the Moon's surface. Eclipses are always powerful benchmarks of change, and most of the time they disrupt and displace people from their familiar and ordinary flow of life. Did you ever read the biblical passage "it rains on the just and the unjust"? This refers to the fact that all of us are affected by celestial phenomena, positively and negatively.

Some astrologers believe that eclipses have less effect on individuals than on aggregate entities—cities and countries, for example, or Wall Street, or Christianity, Catholicism, Islam, or other religions. I disagree. Some who track the stars focus on the negative influences rather than the benefits in everything that happens to us. I have always said that there are no good or bad birth signs; rather it's what you do with the hand life deals you. When given challenges, do you fold your tent or try harder? Do you embrace change or fight modification to the death?

Some charts are more challenging and require more effort to survive than others. Too many things have happened to me and my clients under solar and lunar eclipses to ignore where they are occurring in our personal horoscopes.

Under lunar eclipses, people often experience in their personal lives a sudden end to one pattern and the beginning of a new cycle. For example, a shift may occur in where one works and lives, whether one gets married or divorced, or whether money is plentiful or scarce. On the mundane level, financial markets that have been stagnant or negative might see a more positive economic trend. Movies that favored a certain genre like action adventure will give way to films with a more serious message. The same shift may occur for music and books. One of the major transitions that I see looming is a shift in mass consciousness from a religious to a spiritual orientation, especially when Pluto goes into Capricorn on November 28, 2008.

Just as lunar eclipses are about endings, solar eclipses indicate new beginnings. Three successive solar eclipses set the stage for World War I, and two intense solar eclipses preceded World War II. Just as an architect has precise drawings to design a new building, eclipses are calibrated cosmically in the same way—divine designs that activate planetary configurations in relation to one another to set the stage for an event. In these instances, they were omens of war. The Korean conflict and the fighting in Vietnam started when the planet Mars was in the sign it ruled, Aries, exacerbated by solar eclipses.

There are times of peace and prosperity. Did you live through or read about the Roaring '20s? Did you ever hear about the Great Depression that followed? How about the good times of the '80s and the prosperity of the Bill Clinton presidency? Few of us will forget when the NASDAQ took such a dive and millions of people lost their financial security

I am known as a 24-carat-gold optimist, edified by the cycles and trends and shifts and changes that astrology confirms. What I think helps us most is to understand why we experience health challenges or other difficulties in life. The end of a relationship may be endured as a time of deep suffering by a couple who feel as if their lives are falling apart. But in truth it may turn out to be nothing more than two people who have gone as far as they can go together. I recommend ending an affair or marriage in love. See the benefits of your time together; don't lament the death of the partnership. The same is true for the things we are asked to endure as a democratic fifty states of unity for "life, liberty, and the pursuit of happiness."

As a nation, will we continue to fight, or will we lay down our weapons and make peace? Will we continue to believe that our way is the only way, or will we practice tolerance as many of us did in the '60s and '70s. It is your choice and it is my choice.

Would we choose to change without the threat of catastrophic events? Perhaps not. As I am writing this, I glanced at the headline in *The Arizona Republic:* "Rivers pushed to the brink—Damage caused by decades of growth, neglect and abuse may be irreversible." The article emphasized how we in Arizona have continued to use and abuse the ecosystem so badly that we may run out of water. Everyone hollers *"mea culpa"* over the Iraq War, but it is hard to get many of us to look at how the greatest calamity may be right here at home. My heart tells me that we had better get collaborative and connected in cleaning up and healing our environment or our planetary home may not be habitable too much longer.

As we live through the next few years leading up to 2012, a lot of stressful events will occur in our lives, including more international strife in which warring factions will fight to the death for what they believe to be true. The summers will be hotter and hotter, and the winters will be warmer. Natural disasters will increase in frequency and severity—more destructive hurricanes, more devastating floods and mud slides, more powerful tornadoes. Earthquakes will strike not only in northern and southern California, China, Japan, Turkey, the Middle East and parts of Eastern Europe, but also in places no one is expecting. New dictators will emerge to replace leaders who were working for peace. Nuclear warheads will be deployed on battlefields, and the use of these apocalyptic weapons of mass destruction will elevate fear to an unprecedented level.

So much of what will cause heretofore solid institutions and governments to topple will occur when Pluto goes into Capricorn in 2008. Pluto is associated with the sign of Scorpio and indicates death and elimination. Since Capricorn rules career, reputation, honor, and the larger spheres of power, I predict that when Pluto goes into Capricorn, the United States may begin to see her world esteem and regard tarnished more than it has ever been, and we may begin to see a decline in her reputation as the most powerful country in the world. China and even Russia will emerge as global superpowers that steal much of our thunder, and the glitter that once was America's will shift to these two nations.

Astrologically, the United States of America has been under an ominous cloud of subterfuge, deceit, and double-dealing, which began in November 1998 and will last through December 2012. The planet Neptune, known as the Great Deceiver, has been playing havoc with whom and what we can believe in, because it has afflicted the birth chart of our nation. From Wall Street to all branches of government, most large institutions have breached our faith in them. We ask ourselves, "Whom can I trust? Where are all the half-truths and outright lies leading this country? Can we recover from the miasma of these deceptions, and when?" Combined with the malicious influence of Pluto the Great Destroyer playing havoc with our country's birth chart as well, we are in for a lot of painful and angst-ridden times.

But I am the optimist, remember. We will survive, and we will persevere. The United States of America has healed and reunited after a civil war, survived a stock market crash that led to the Great Depression, had the courage to face civil injustices toward minorities, bounced back from the betrayal we felt throughout the Watergate scandal, and hopefully is resolved not to allow the terrorist attacks on September 11 to undermine the Bill of Rights and the Constitution.

I found an interesting article by Hector Carreon of the controversial online newspaper, *La Voz de Aztlan*. Carreon concluded that the knowledge the Mayans received after ingesting the awareness-enhancing plant peyote allowed them to ascertain what is going to happen by December 21, 2012 . Plant-derived insights also revealed to them what would happen on specific dates now past.

According to Carreon's research, the Mayans were deeply spiritual and very aware of the role that human consciousness plays in connecting to and obtaining information from nature. They knew that ingesting these plants, religiously and with reverence, would open the doors of perception and lift the veil that keeps mankind from seeing certain realities and communicating with God.

Since I have an allergy of the body coupled with an obsession of the mind regarding mind-altering substances like peyote, I must be crystal clear enough to use my own intuition to glean what the Divine says to me about anything I need to share with you. I say that because I don't recommend the use of any mind-altering plants to enhance intuition. A good reason is that I am a recovering addict and alcoholic. I am not Mayan, and I did not live in the time when the calendar was designed and interpreted.

I am reminded of Carlos Castaneda, who wrote *The Teachings of Don Juan: A Yaqui Way of Knowledge,* in which he described his training in traditional Native American shamanism, a form of "sorcery", under the influence of psychoactive drugs like peyote. Castaneda was wildly popular with readers for the insights he gave them through his experiences.

The Mayans were gifted astrologers and astronomers and used the movement of the planets to predict the future. They possessed the required knowledge to use what the movement of the stars was telling them—which they have been able to do for centuries—to come to the conclusion that December 21, 2012 is the end of the Mayan calendar. Dr. Carl Johan Calleman, author of *The Mayan Calendar* (Garev, 2001) and *The Mayan Calendar and the Transformation of Consciousness* (Bear and Co., 2004), writes that by his calculations the end of the Mayan calendar is to be October 28, 2011.

It is not my purpose to educate you about the Mayan calendar or to debate dates, but rather to let you know what I believe will happen and why. What's a year, give or take? You will soon find out that it's never a specific date but all the things we do or don't do that will lead us to enlightenment or keep us in darkness.

Dr. Calleman has studied the Mayan civilization since 1979 when, as an environmental toxicologist, he visited Mexico and Guatemala and became drawn to the Mayan culture. Eventually he studied its lost civilization and the Mayan calendar. He made some startling pronouncements in a paper he wrote on July 27, 2006, entitled *On Israel and Islam: Updates on the Approach to the*

Fifth Day of the Galactic Underworld. He concludes that Mayan prophecy, based upon calendrical calculations, says that the war between the Muslims and the Jews will escalate to include other nations throughout the region as we approach the dates for the end of the Mayan calendar, whichever date you choose. Many deaths, as well as obliteration of cities and towns, will occur in the name of God.

I agree with the good doctor when he says that "Fundamentalist Christians, especially in the United States, are not indifferent to this conflict and in fact see the scenario playing out as verifying their own prophecies, which is part of the reason for the strong U.S. backing of Israel. These groups expect the Jews to rebuild the temple, following which there will be great tribulations that will lead the Jews to accept Jesus as their Messiah. The Muslims on their part expect the appearance of the twelfth imam, Mahdi, as a savior, as well as the return of Jesus, who will lead the Christians to submit to Islam."

The catastrophic warmongering going on in the world now, and which apparently will escalate, can be traced to the influence that left-brain reasoning has held over countries under the spell of religious fundamentalism, as it does in Muslim countries, as well as in Israel. It applies to the religious right in this country, as well. Left-brain consciousness must be fused and balanced with the right half of the brain, which allows one to have visions and see images and catch the wave of what is silent and invisible, or the world will never know peace. Absence of this balance leads to bully leadership and worse—dictators or presidents who reign, rather than lead their people. Left-brain consciousness for itself alone without integration with right brain is testosterone amped way up.

I have always said that you need to take your power back; read scriptures, but do not allow the minister to tell you what the verses mean. Your right brain might tell you something different than his left brain. The secret to surviving dogmatic fundamentalism is to have your own relationship with the Divine.

Sam Harris in his book *The End of Faith: Religion, Terror, and the Future of Reason* (W.W. Norton, 2004) makes the case for why faith itself is the most dangerous element of modern life. He says that any belief system that speaks with assurance about the hereafter has the potential to place far less value on the here and now. He asks us to consider that those who do not fear death for themselves, and who also revere ancient scriptures instructing them to mete it out generously to others, may soon have these weapons in their hands.

Dr. Calleman asserts that the Mayan calendar does not predict any particular eventuality within a specific time period. He also says that the intuition and life experiences of the prognosticator influence his predictions.

Excuse me, but have we not had a turbulent world since Adam bit the apple? There have always been calamities. The victims of hurricane Katrina have already had their apocalypse, in a sweltering stadium with no privacy and not enough food, water or toilets. From the rooftops of their homes and in the flotsam-infested water that did not recede for weeks, they may have wished they were dead. Earthquakes have killed hundreds of thousands of people. Floods have destroyed cities and villages and their peoples. Tornadoes have wiped out towns and killed hundreds.

Have we not had wars and rumors of war since the caveman crafted a club? The worst catastrophes have been wars waged in the name of God, when the real reason for one country to invade another is to control its resources, like gold or oil, or to impose its will on a people who want to be free. True, there are occasional quiet periods when the warlords take a break, but in general man always seems to be fighting somebody over something, usually in the name of God.

You can talk about peace as much as you want. You can go to spiritual conclaves and conferences and listen to all the powder-puff hocus-pocus speeches in the world, but unless each of us changes the way we live and the way we think—including admitting that our God is not the only God—we *will* go up in smoke; the world *will* end with a whimper, or, more likely, a bang. If warring nations do not change how they view their God and their tenets and their prophecies, and allow everyman to worship God as he sees fit, we are toast. The movie ends.

In the midst of this research, I received an unsolicited e-mail that directed me to the Mayan Calendar Code website (**www.mayan-calendar-code.com**). This synchronistic coincidence both amplified and simplified my search and confirmed my understanding of the whole Mayan calendar business.

Basically, this site says that you and I are part of a global picture show—a divine design to open wider the doors of our universal consciousness. (They distinguish personal consciousness with a little "c" and global Consciousness with a capital "C"). The creators of the site believe that our world is not only in overload with random acts of violence, but it is simultaneously in a countdown to resolution of wars, famine, violence, man's inhumanity to man, and all other horrible suffering. For the light to conquer the dark, what is required of each of us is to draw from the intelligence and forecasts of the Mayan calendar, which provide the lay lines to hook up with this global consciousness.

The calendar contains 13 tones and 20 glyphs (day signs), which total 260 days in a Mayan year. Interestingly, humans are the only creatures with 260 different cell types in our bodies, and the gestation period of a human child is slightly more than 260 days. My intuition opened me to the possibility that the Mayan calendar—like our astrological birth chart—is encoded *within* us at birth. Having a personal calendar that receives mind-to-mind signals from higher consciousness aligns with my philosophy that all of the answers are within us. In other words, no matter what the conjecture about which official calendar is the more accurate, Mayan or Gregorian, the one that counts is the one encoded within us at birth. Whereas the Gregorian calendar gives us sterile dates in a day planner, the Mayan calendar, as I perceive it, brings alive the true purpose of life on Earth and what we are facing if we don't change.

Just as our fingerprints identify us and we cannot escape who our DNA says we are, it is my own personal revelation that each of us *is* the Mayan calendar.

The world in which we live, made worse by each of us over time, is not headed for death, destruction, and global genocide, unless we fail to change our intent. And although 2012 is a timeline when we will reap what we have sown, now is turnaround time, not 2011 or 2012. As with the Harmonic Convergence, no colossal event will take place on a specific date; we should open our eyes to what we don't do leading up to the ground-zero dateline. Look at the landscape in your own neighborhood and in the world at large. We don't need Nostradamus to prophesy our fate; our destruction or salvation is in our own hands.

There is time to change, and we must change the world by changing ourselves. We must feed the poor and share water and other geophysical assets to ensure that our brothers and sisters are taken care of.

I have suggested to clients and friends, when they ask me what they can do to get ready for the shift in consciousness, that they practice dying. Yes, practice dying. I tell them they should do so by meditating at such a deep level that they think they are dead.

Death is a good place to leave behind what is not working and what blocks your transformation. When you lie down to sleep, close your eyes and breathe deeply, and embrace a very special dream space where the Divine lives. Practice dying to all the material things you have overvalued: the jewelry and clothes you wear, the car you drive, the house you live in, and all the money you have amassed. You may be called upon to let go of a lot of it or all of it anyway. Practice dying to the "my God is the only God" belief system. Practice dying to all the hurtful and divisive and self-centered thoughts through which your ego controls everything you do and say.

The United States is responsible for 30% of global warming, more than Central and South America and the Middle East put together. We pollute and we use more water and more natural resources than should be our allotment. If we think of ourselves as the world's mightiest nation, ought we not to lead the world in toxic clean-up and sharing generously of what we have?

This research convinced me that the worldview must shift from one in which the United States is seen as a self-serving superpower to one in which America is once again known by her actions as a land of compassion and concern for the world community. We must stop beating our chests and start embracing our neighbors, sharing what we have to give. The wealth of the United States alone could change a world starving and thirsty and dying from AIDS to one of sufficiency for our brothers and sisters.

I read documents that reaffirmed that we human beings are merely fluid energy—electrical currents—in a dimension much denser than the other worlds in our galaxy. I was relieved when one scientist admitted that he didn't know as much as the layman credited him with knowing. "The galactic mysteries may always remain a conundrum," he said. One article I read online pointed out how we can get information from a source that seems to be free-floating and illogical but turns out to be an unexpectedly accurate reflection of how things really are. I loved the reports that talked about intuition and tuning into one's personal physics.

I took all this information to mean that to avert dire consequences, we can change ourselves. Change yourself to change the world.

Christian end-time prophecies have been around longer than Methuselah, and I still won't let them hold me hostage. I do not fear the future that radical fundamentalists claim awaits us non-believers. They have distorted and lied to good churchgoers for millennia. I have read *The Decline and Fall of the Roman Empire* by Edward Gibbon, and I know that history repeats itself. I am more interested in what I am willing to start doing today to atone for the ways I have contributed to the devolution of the world. As Paul points out, I need to change me.

My research reconfirmed the idea that answers and questions are in the same place—within each of us. Astrology has always been about timing. Swami had said that when it was time for my life to change, the road would bend and I would follow it. The road is bending for all of us.

The most astounding piece of new news I picked up was hiding in plain sight: Mankind has returned to Earth or the Lower World to rectify words and deeds from this and other incarnations, and once these transgressions are faced, a homing resonance—an intuitive entrance into what has been hidden from us before—will be revealed. It is time for mankind to change frequencies; it is time for us to see how our world of materialism must transmute into a more selfless consciousness. What is ahead will be as difficult as we make it or as harmonious as our actions can create.

Are we going to continue to act out of self-interest, or will we begin to recognize that we are global citizens who must look after the welfare of one other? Is reaching out to offer part of our resources to people in distress whom we don't know—who worship a different God and whose government is not democratic—one of the steps to becoming who we really are?

Richard Tarnas, graduate of Harvard University and founding director of the Philosophy, Cosmology, and Consciousness graduate program at the California Institute of Integral Studies in San Francisco, writes about the challenges that face mankind in *Cosmos and Psyche: Intimations of a New World View.* Tarnas states, "One need not be graced with prophetic insight to recognize that we are living in one of those rare ages, like the end of classical antiquity or the beginning of the modern era, that bring forth, through great stress and struggle, a genuinely fundamental transformation in the underlying assumptions and principles of the cultural worldview. The outcome of this tremendous moment in our civilization's history is deeply uncertain. Something is dying and something is being reborn. The stakes are high for the future of humanity and the future of the earth."

I turned off my computer. I wanted some confirmation about my research. Satisfied that I was in control of my life and that no negative force or source could influence me without my say-so, I decided to stay another night in Birmingham, to assimilate all the information Paul was helping me remember. I made a few calls and booked a flight for the next night.

After four or five minutes in silence and using my breathing exercise, he spoke.

I am going to help you remember what you have always known, but illusion has caused you to forget.

"Will you answer questions as you teach me how to clear?" I asked.

Our relationship will be as simple as retrieving information from a computer when you know the password.

"Do you have any suggestions about how to prepare for the end of the Mayan calendar in 2012?"

Discover who you are. Revelations will appear as you need to know them. Do what you are doing. Stay the course. Whatever you do, do not get stuck in trying to figure out what the end of the Mayan calendar means—let it be revealed when the time is right. Do not get waylaid by giving energy to the destruction that may lie ahead. If you don't like weeds, pull them out by their roots. If you like flowers, give them water and feed them nutrients. If you want peace, make peace.

It seems like planet Earth is going to face a lot of natural disasters as we head toward 2012.

You have an expression that explains your dilemma. Planet Earth has made its bed, and now must lie in it. Or you might consider changing your bed. It all depends on what like-minded people can do to un-create what you have done to pollute and harm one another.

"Why do I still have a lot of fear?" I asked.

You fear yourself. From the time you were a little boy you knew that what you heard and saw with your five senses was not real. You knew that what you were trained to believe was not true. Your unconscious was trying to tell you that one day you would know the truth.

Instantly I recalled my childhood. I was born with club feet and spent a lot of time being coddled by doctors and nurses. When I finally came home to live with my parents and siblings, I thought I was in the wrong house. Where were the servants? Why were we so poor? I heard voices and I saw dead people. I knew things no one else did. I had no one to mentor me. I was a stranger in a strange land.

Poverty can be overcome, and it was. It was Christianity that left the deepest scars. One cold and rainy winter Sunday night at the Baptist church, your pastor said, "Tonight one of you sinners is going to burn in hell." You thought he was talking about you. You were just ten years old.

Psychologist Carl Gustav Jung did not attend church although his father was a minister. He did, however, believe in a higher power and wrote that to be healthy and happy one must believe in a supreme being.

"Many books challenge Jesus and his crucifixion; one says Judas was chosen by Christ to betray him. Are these accounts true or false?" I asked.

You have said for many years that Judas was a high master who was cast in the role of the betrayer of Christ, much as an actor would accept a part in a play. He lives in infamy as a hated man. You need to remember that it takes a selfless soul to incarnate as one as reviled as Judas.

Stories of teachers were written to excite people about redemption, but too much attention is paid to the personalities rather than to the lessons the stories teach. You discovered the ego in the church, the state and even science. Reeducate your ego and you can enjoy myths, legends, and biblical stories for the insights they provide.

Would Jesus's teachings have been less true had he not died on the cross?

In recovery circles, we are wont to say "principles before personalities." We live in a culture that is so enamored of personalities that we don't look to see who a person is or what he stands for. To my way of thinking, Jesus's teachings stand the test of time. They are truths by which many of us live our lives. Only institutionalized religion has made belief in the man tantamount to "being saved." I personally don't believe that whether or not Jesus died on the cross is important. His teachings are what are profoundly important.

An early Christian manuscript, including the only text of what is known as the Gospel of Judas, has surfaced after 1,700 years," reported the *New York Times*. The discovery in Egypt of the leather-bound papyrus relates the account of Jesus telling Judas that he will exceed all of Christ's disciples because "you will sacrifice the man that clothes me," meaning that he would help Jesus shed his physical flesh.

The Nag Hammadi library, a collection of thirteen ancient codices containing more than fifty texts, including the Gospel of Thomas, the Gospel of Philip, and the Gospel of Truth, was discovered in Upper Egypt in 1945. The discovery and translation of the Nag Hammadi library, completed in the 1970s, has provided impetus for a major reevaluation of early Christian history and the nature of gnosticism.

Gnosis is esoteric knowledge of the oneness of God and self essential to salvation. Such a direct approach to God requires no intermediary—after all, God is the spirit and light within. A Gnostic rabbi did not preside over a temple and dispense religious truths; rather, people had to become initiated into the Gnostic order. The foundation of their belief was that matter is evil and emancipation comes through gnosis.

In 1947, young Bedouin shepherds found jars filled with ancient scrolls carbon-dated to 68 C.E., which changed the view of ancient Judaism popularized by the King James Bible. These came to be known as the Dead Sea Scrolls, chronicles of a time when Jesus of Nazareth lived, and they are older than any surviving biblical manuscripts by almost a thousand years.

Elaine Pagels, a professor of religion at Princeton who specializes in studies of the Gnostics, said, "These discoveries are exploding the myth of a monolithic religion, and demonstrating how diverse—and fascinating—the early Christian movement was."

"Paul, are we Gnostics awakening to remember what we have always known?"

There is a resurgence of gnosis and a decline in religion. People want to be self-legislated. People do not want to follow man-made rules and regulations. Mankind is looking for a personal relationship with God. Legalism is dying as spiritualism is being resurrected.

Do not be concerned about controversies. The ego of the church and its myths are being discredited by documents being unearthed. What is true and what is real is that God is within you, and He has a plan for your life. Serve God and you serve man. Be guided by ego and you will die with regret. Your world is transitory. The ego makes a lot of promises that it cannot keep. Play the ego game and you will end up as the ego—shamed for the price you paid to live in illusion.

Shards of truth are found in a desert cave; an imperial burial ground is discovered six feet under; and codes are cracked at the right time for mankind to remember. Put the findings together and you have a puzzle that contains a startling revelation.

Astrology gives you the times for discovery and why. As a child in the first grade cannot remember what a student in the tenth grade can, mankind is at varying levels of remembrance.

The stars are part of a sky-map mystery. Specific planetary movements, such as Pluto changing signs from Sagittarius to Capricorn, or solar and lunar eclipses, portend a coming spiritual renaissance. Man is awakening as he really is. Watch the heavens—decipher celestial movement. Signs of providential change are written in the puzzles in the sky.

"Why is there so much war?" I asked.

Man is at war with himself. He struggles to reconnect to who he really is. Man's ego causes war to spill out into streets, battlefields, boardrooms, and bedrooms.

39

Christ, Buddha, Ramakrishna, and many other revered teachers sacrificed themselves so that they could bring enlightenment to man. But man loves darkness more than he wants to be enlightened.

"How can I influence people?"

Remember the pyramid. Redemption begins with one person who shares with someone else. Everybody above and below is connected by the two principles of sound and light.

Paul had told me that we are all fallen angels. I found it hard to believe that someone evil can be an angel. Dark souls include terrorists, war hawks, and greedy Wall Street tycoons who have little concern for those who suffer. I needed for Paul to explain how these people could be angels.

You mentioned evidence that Judas was appointed by Jesus to betray him, yet history painted him as evil. Like Jesus, Judas had the spark of the divine within him. With time, the truth of who Judas was changed. Perhaps one viewed as dark today may prove in time to be working with the light.

Look within your own akashic record for your answer, Albert. You have lived many depraved lives, yet today you help others. The cosmic system of karmic retribution joined natural law to offer you redemption. You are on the right path now, but you lived a ruthless life as a soldier in France, another as a demagogue in Russia, and another as a corrupt barrister in England. When you can look honestly at yourself, you will be able to remember all these lives. You must remember in order to make amends and to change. All memory of past lives is within you.

Paul said that a soul must atone for its mistakes by facing "shadow blocks" to his or her true identity. Shadow blocks are confusions that arise when a soul neither male nor female comes to Earth and assumes a gender. We do not know how to act with integrity as the divided self. Women unconsciously transfer unwanted qualities onto men, and men do the same to women. This confusion does not allow us to be who we are; we are masculine and feminine.

Albert, welcome to the school of remembering. Knowing is born within you. You never learn anything, you remember.

Telepathy signaled you to look for information from teachers and authorities regarding the year 2012. Your intuition did the rest.

When I need to remember something, the sourcebook appears right in front of me, or it pops up on an Internet search.

Paul then proceeded to explain to me what happened in the beginning of time, when we were all one. He told me that after the fall we were split apart, divided and separated from original Oneness. Through millennia and lifetimes, man has forgotten who he really is. In the beginning of time, we existed without physical form. And because the rate of vibration was so accelerated beyond what we can comprehend today, we communicated without words—through mind-to-mind transmission. In our galaxy, specifically on Earth, in order to have physical form and to engage our five senses and to speak as we do, the rate of vibration slows down. Earth has the lowest rate of vibration of any planet in any galaxy.

Mythology says that the dark side, known to us as the Devil, had an irreconcilable conflict with God that led to a split in the Upper World. The Devil left Paradise and took with him other angels. This is where we get the expression fallen angel.

We are all attempting to reconvene in the spirit of original union. We must not let fear keep us from beginning the journey home. Ego tries to convince us that High Self wants to harm us.

High Self is a guidance system that resonates with our level of clearing.

"Paul, all of this seems like a rainbow of miracles. It is as if the Divine has intervened in my life, giving me a new way to live and love and comprehend who I am."

The beauty of miracles, Albert, is that you have been able to transcend the limitations of your Earth dimension. The beauty of miracles is the awakening—the remembrance of things as they truly are meant to be—the breaking with illusion. You are beginning the journey of the discovery of your true self. Miracles are for everyone who can see them and feel them as you have. Mankind is receiving what has been in storage for millennia.

Having looked at separation and emptiness, people must make a decision to make amends for their behavior. All who want to reconnect to their authentic selves will be able to activate a homing effect, the pitch and octave of which will allow them to recognize themselves as precious children of God.

You are intrigued with mystery and buried treasure. You seek to discover the hall of records and to uncover the Holy Grail. Better you should ask the question, "Who am I?"

To begin the return home, know that the hall of records—where you have been and where you need to return—is buried within you, not under the sphinx or on a remote mountaintop. Your guru told you the Sufi legend of creation and where to put God. The hall of records is where God is, within man.

On your many trips to Egypt and Greece—two of your ancient homes—sound and light shows helped you remember when you were there in other lives. Mysteries are revealed through sound waves and light emanations. Reconnect to what is true about you and the world in which you live. That truth is more easily revealed when you are silent and contemplative while in meditation.

Listen to the resonance of the sound one makes, then watch his aura. By his sound and his light, you will know who he is and how aligned he is with what you know and your purpose for being here.

You always were and you always will be. You have been a part of crusades to help the planet return to God, and you have also helped create the pollution, greed, poverty, racial strife, manipulation, warmongering, and other heinous acts that have kept the planet in darkness.

At the moment of the terrorists' attacks on the twin towers of the World Trade Center on September 11, 2001, I was in New York. I turned to my business partner and asked, "What have I done to create this?" I know that we are part of a collective unconscious that creates all good and all evil in the world.

You are a sensitive man who feels and sees beneath what someone says or does. You do not operate in the world as others do. You detect primal cause. Although you live in the mundane world, you are attuned to the continuum of events. When the terrorists attacked the United States, you knew that some time, somewhere you had been as they are now. You have been on the side of death and destruction, and you recognized yourself in the enemy. You live in a culture that is selfish and greedy and blames others. Mankind is at a place in the devolution of the planet where it must take responsibility for what it has created.

As a sober man, you must give away what you have found; help others to see the light and to take the steps to return to their real selves. As you have shed your own false disguises, you will help others remove their masks. You will guide them to face down the great egocentric deceiver and free the precious children of God buried in the rubble of their destructive actions.

"You have talked about being equally yoked—not getting on the path with those whose intentions are less aligned with spirit than mine. Are we attracted or repelled by the sound of someone's voice?" I asked.

Yes. This phenomenon is called imprinting. Hear a man's voice and you will like him immediately or want to flee his presence. You will have an inner confirmation as to whether the person in question is in alignment with your own soul matrix.

All world leaders have the power of resonance. Many use their voices with positive results. Actors, teachers, politicians, industrialists, and ministers sway people. Adolf Hitler, Benito Mussolini, Josef Stalin, and many others were calibrated with the message of darkness.

Slowly I awakened on my bed, much like a deep-sea diver surfaces. I stretched and yawned and hopped out of bed. In order to capture what I had experienced, I recorded in my journal all the insights from Paul.

Chapter 3

Dreams and Daydreams

I telephoned a good friend, Rick Pate, known to be a doubting Thomas. He is a forty-something executive who had signed up for my Egypt trip. We talked a few minutes about the mysticism of the Nile valley. I told him to enjoy Egypt, one of the world's most intriguing countries, but never to drink the water or eat uncooked vegetables or fruit served without its rind.

"Rick, when you consult with me, where do you think I get my information?"

"I never gave it much thought, but your insights have always been accurate," he answered.

"I am intuitive. Where does that come from?" I inquired.

"You are a channeler," he answered.

"You are wrong. I am connected to a source, but it's no entity," I stated firmly.

If I leave one footprint in the sands of time, it is "don't give your power away." Channeling smacks of unquestioned authority.

There was silence on the other end of the phone. I could tell I had offended Rick.

"I should not have overreacted, Rick. Something intriguing happened to me today and I needed to tell someone about it," I said.

I told Rick about Paul. I said that I had not a scintilla of doubt about Paul's information. But it was difficult to explain how Paul was not an entity.

Rick helped with his insights. "You have found a source of inspiration. I booked my first session after I heard you lecture. You said that astrology was a road map for life but not gloom and doom or pie-in-the-sky prophecy. You said what I do with my planetary energies was the value of having my chart read."

"Do you understand what part of me Paul is? Do you understand that each of us has High Self guidance?"

"Albert, I learned a big lesson from you a while ago: Faith, not facts, is a better way to live. You advised me to learn to listen to my own still, small voice. Paul sounds like your voice of intuition. When we hang up I am going to see if I can make contact with my High Self."

Rick wanted to talk about the Mayan calendar. He told me that his chldhood preacher had scared the bejesus out of him for years about the end of the world, Christ coming back in a blaze of glory after years of war, famine, and pestilence. Gradually he had opened up to metaphysics.

"In plain-Jane language, Albert, what do you think is going to happen in 2012?" Rick asked.

"My hunch is that the planet is about to reach critical mass— our actions collectively are going to expose us to natural and man-made disasters. Each of us is going to go through a consciousness purge. Part of that cleansing may involve cataclysms necessary to wake us up to true self and how we are destroying the world. Man will change through instruction from himself. And the purge involves lessons that will awaken us to repudiate everything that separates us," I said.

"What do you mean by clearing?" Rick asked.

"Being less whom I think I am and more who God created me to be," I answered. "You're not who you think you are, Rick, and things are not what they seem."

As we said our good-byes, I noticed a phone message under the door that reconfirmed my hotel reservations at the San Ysidro Ranch in Montecito, California. I decided that I needed a good night's sleep with no Paul and no new information. As stimulating and profound as this awakening to Paul and his lessons were, I just wanted to rest. I fell asleep easily and slept soundly.

The next morning a dream had so perplexed me that I needed some help understanding it. Through time I learned that once I had made contact with Paul, he was always there, and I could draw information from that part of me that Paul represents.

I began to breathe gently and smoothly, taking deep breaths and exhaling slowly. A familiar voice greeted me as I felt all tension leave my body.

Albert, your dream reminded you to stay in the present and not in the past. Explore and discover, but do not lose sight of what needs to be done in the moment.

"Why do we dream?"

Dreams and daydreams and catnapping reconnect you to people or situations that may be coming back into your life through the law of attraction. Dreams oftentimes foreshadow unfinished business or amends to be made. You encounter a situation you have been in before; now you can handle it differently. Dreams and coincidences are connected. You may dream of a person and meet him in your awakened consciousness. Dreams release chaos stored in the unconscious, and they autosuggest lessons you need to learn. They are enlightening, and they educate your dark side. Dreams are real. Your waking reality is unreal. Dreams have a life of their own and are teaching tools for life's problems.

Dreams are often connected to a past or future life. Past lives are a part of the collective unconscious that you are learning to access, like taking valuables from a safe deposit box. After you die you go to reform school in the Upper World and are shown your mistakes. Then you are born again to live a life with greater integrity.

Dreams highlight changes that need to be made in how you think and how you act. They are inducements to remember. When you sleep, you are disconnected from your busy, frenetic pace. The nature of the dream state is such that you must let go of all control dramas. You don't choose from a menu what movie you want to watch. You are more receptive to dreams because you are powerless to change them.

Symbols and signs affect what happens when you wake up from a dream. If your dream was foreboding, you will get out of bed with trepidation. If your dream was pleasant, you will feel uplifted. Certain signs or symbols indicate an area of your life that needs attention. Dreams are a way of helping you without interference.

Many years ago I took classes in dream interpretation called "Wake Up, You're Dreaming," with lifelong Sedona resident Jaine Smith. She taught us to remember our dreams in three simple steps:

1) As you are falling to sleep, repeat over and over the question you want answered in a dream. For example: Where am I supposed to move? 2) Take a bath or shower before retiring for the night. Make sure your sheets are fresh and clean'3) Place a glass

of water bedside. Drinking water upon awakening from a dream enhances recall. 4) Put a tape or CD recorder with voice-activated capability on the table next to your bed. If you wake up from a dream in the middle of the night you can record it effortlessly. As an alternative to using a recorder, put a pencil and paper by your bed so you can write down your dream when you wake up.

You are the only one who can interpret your dreams. Dream interpretation books are misleading. Use your intuition to know what a dream tells you.

Everyone dreams, and all dreams are relevant. No matter who shows up in your dream, it's your dream—it's about you. If you dream about someone whom you feel is vain, look at your own vanity. Some dreams are instructional while others are entertaining. A dream can be an omen with a message of caution. When you can't remember your dreams, don't fret. You are processing and eliminating at an unconscious level, where all master work is done.

"Why do I always dream about forgetting my locker number at school, just when I am to take a test in the classroom?" I asked. "When I reach the class, I have just missed the exam."

Like tying a string on your finger, this repetitive dream reminds you that you still have a lot to learn. The inability to remember your locker number emphasizes that you don't know who you are—keep digging. Missing an examination indicates that you are avoiding a harsh lesson.

"Paul, what are dreams trying to tell us?" I asked.

The curriculum of the school of life states that you must return to Earth in service to others, and to atone for past deeds. Dreams aid the process of knowing how to make amends from present and past incarnations. Dreams can help accelerate your spiritual progress.

Paul told me that soon I would be able to interpret dreams and comprehend lesson-recall information and data. Dreams are like traffic cops on the avenue, giving us directions.

In Paulo Coelho's international best seller, *The Alchemist*, Santiago, a shepherd boy journeys from Spain to Morocco in search of worldly success, and eventually to Egypt, where a fateful encounter with an alchemist brings him at last to self-understanding and spiritual enlightenment. Along the way an old gypsy woman tells Santiago "dreams are the language of God. When he speaks in our language, I can interpret what he has to say. But if he speaks in the language of the soul, it is only you who can understand."

Paul then shared something that cleared up many questions about my relationship with him. The Earth-bound Albert must deal with karma, and I will reap the effects of what I have sown in this life and before. The High Self is the part of me that can lead the way back to the Upper World. Paul leads the way, and I follow.

To strengthen your spiritual nature, repeat words like angel, love, light, redemption, transcendence, joy, peace, balance, harmony, rapture, truth, and beauty. They alter the energy of an interaction and soothe personal relationships. These words carry alchemical harmonics that can still troubled waters.

Dr. Masaru Emoto wrote in his *New York Times* best-seller, *The Hidden Messages in Water,* that molecules of water are affected by our thoughts, words, and feelings. Since humans and the Earth are composed mostly of water, his message is one of personal health, global environmental renewal, and a practical plan for peace that starts with each of us. Dr. Emoto suggests that you invoke the highest good for someone if you end a letter with "Love and Gratitude."

Remember what I told you about the beauty of miracles. Your breakthrough to truth and the real self—the authentic self—is the ultimate miracle of life. And the beauty of a miracle is that you did not have to travel the world to find this elusive Holy Grail. The miracle is to be found within you.

Santiago, the shepherd boy in *The Alchemist,* travels to Egypt to find his buried treasure, but returns to Andalusia empty-handed. Inspired by thought impression in a dream, he digs up a chest of Spanish gold coins in an abandoned church back home.

"You old sorcerer," the boy shouted up to the sky. "You knew the whole story. Couldn't you have saved me from that?"

He heard a voice on the wind say, "No, if I had told you, you wouldn't have seen the pyramids."

Fallen angels who take the path back to God through a soul cleansing will be given the power to heal others. Miracle healing will have nothing to do with alchemy, potions, elixirs, talismans, or voodoo. Through the restored soul, the power of healing will come through as currents on a wire or a voice over a phone.

But you may choose to ignore your High Self guidance. It will make return to God slower and rougher, but High Self must stand back and wait for you to accept help. You are children who have slipped into eternal forgetfulness. You have forgotten who you are.

Paul taught me that I am being hypnotized by desire: desire for sex, food, alcohol, drugs, cars, clothes, money, and material possessions that try to make up for my separation from God.

When a kid at summer camp is homesick, the counselor takes the camper on a hike, swimming, or horseback riding to make him forget home. The ego keeps us drugged with things so we forget who we are and where we come from.

Paul advised me that soon I would no longer have to be in meditation or in an altered state to access information or to remember what I was to do. The message and the messenger would become the same.

The period of Ego's dominance is ending, and God's light will grow brighter. The year 2012 is when millions of souls will have migrated back to God. Those who do not return will continue to live with an unchanged consciousness. They will live with no hope. Because of negative force fields, it took a long time for the power of memory to strengthen on Earth. Darkness continues not only from wars that nations wage against one another, but also from the war that rages within man.

The End of Sorrow by Eknath Easwaran is a commentary on the Bhagavad Gita, a Hindu bible, which says that the war is always within us and the wisdom of God is within us as well. Whenever you're disturbed, you are the problem. Pain has been an effective tool to take us deep within ourselves to remember who we really are.

You will encounter lessons to lead you back home to God. You are entitled to see everything that has gone on in the past. To know the past is to know the future.

Life is like a giant Chinese puzzle. The more you clear, the more you will know. Stay stuck in the ego, and you will never return home. You return a degree at a time, a step at a time. You could make the journey faster, but your ego uses doubt and fear to deceive you. Use the dream state to guide your choices. Not all souls have the deep desire for redemption. Many are on assignment to serve the dark side of the unconscious. Use discernment when you share the light. Seek the higher ground, and you will be guided by a power greater than yourself.

There was a moment of silence.

Man loves darkness rather than light.

My work was finished in Birmingham, but my life's mission was just beginning. As I packed for the airport, a lot of questions danced in my head. Why had I felt all my life that I had little connection to my family? Why did I choose alcoholism as a means to get back to God? How can we be someone other than who we are? Have I been living in a drama that made me face karma before I could get to my true purpose in life?

The answers were apparently to be found within myself by means of intuition. The reason I could not know the answer to the question "Who am I?" was that my ego had camouflaged my true identity with lies. I was ready to find true purpose for my life.

Chapter 4

The Ego Is Not the Enemy

The San Ysidro Ranch in Montecito, California, is a popular weekend retreat for the idle rich and famous actors, writers, and producers who love to drink downstairs at the Plow and Angel Bar before they go upstairs for a scrumptious dinner at the restaurant. Locals love the food so much it's hard for guests at the Ranch to get a table. Originally owned by British-born actor Ronald Colman who starred in such film classics as *The Light that Failed,* the San Ysidro Ranch is nestled in the Santa Ynez Mountains two miles from the Pacific Ocean and 100 miles north of Los Angeles. The ranch is idyllic for writing. It was restored in 1976 by Jim Lavenson, former president of the Plaza Hotel in New York, and his peripatetic wife, pistol-ball Susie. I found this gem in 1978 when I sold actor John Travolta a 35-acre Spanish-land-grant estate abutting Ronald Reagan's property near Gaviota Beach. I babysat the transaction at the San Ysidro Ranch. I also wrote a motion picture there, a reincarnation love story entitled *The World Is Waiting.*

The Vedanta Society maintains the Sarada Convent on Montecito's Ladera Lane and a monastery a few miles from the Ranch. There, I worship in the temple, visit with the nuns over lunch, and counsel with Swami Swahananda.

I arrived at the ranch on a Saturday afternoon and settled into my favorite cottage, Outlook III, where Somerset Maugham wrote *The Razor's Edge.*

I took a walk through the gardens with a mineral water in one hand and my tape recorder in the other. Hiking higher into the hills, I lay down on my favorite rock overlooking the swimming pool and turned on the tape recorder and sat it next to my head. I wanted to record to remember what I heard.

Balmy breezes blew in from the ocean as I sank deeper and deeper into that peaceful place where I communicate with Paul.

The message and the messenger will become the same.

Lesson 1:

The Ego Is Not the Enemy

In my own understanding of the word, the ego was how I interacted with the world to satisfy my own desires. Sometimes my ego served me well. It helped me make my way in the world in a fair and conscientious manner. But for most of my adult life my ego had gotten way out of control. And those were the times I had gotten into trouble, big trouble.

I have always been a fan of Joseph Campbell, a transpersonal psychologist and author, whose thinking was very influenced by the theories of Freud and Jung. Joseph Campbell had touched on the subject of ego in his mythological version of how the Earth was created. In *The Power of Myth,* Campbell describes the rebellion of Lucifer and his minions, how they left paradise and set up camp on Earth, which God had set aside for these outcasts. To stay in the Order of Lucifer, fallen angels took a vow never to say the name of God. Campbell contended that all of us are fallen angels, separated from God by lawless egos, and that our redemption can only come by speaking to God directly and learning to make better choices.

Looking back at my own life, I had to admit that despite all of my conventional religious training I never really felt connected to God. Quite the opposite. Ever since I was a little boy, I often felt lonely and afraid. If I had to be honest with myself, I'd admit fear was the primary emotion that drove me. Much like Edgar Bergen's dummy, Charlie McCarthy, I had been doing what my ego drove me to do out of some misguided idea that this would bring peace and control. In the absence of true spirituality, my ego had taken charge of me, helping to create a life of illusion and deception woven around addictions. The authentic me, the child of God, had been pushed to the background.

This was an interesting paradox to me. A healthy ego is important not only to survive but also to flourish in the world, but it can sabotage. I understood I needed to rein my ego in, but how? And then it dawned on me; like two kids whose ankles are tied together in a foot race, my ego and I must cooperate, work together to find a balance. As this thought crossed my mind, I remembered a verse I had learned as a boy at church, "Out of the depths I cry to thee, Lord hear my prayer, let thine ears be attended to the voice of thy supplicant." I would cry out and then I would listen. And what I would hear would guide me.

The ego is not an evil entity to be destroyed or avoided but a valuable aspect of us that needs to be reeducated. Unconscious and without boundaries, the ego is the part of our self that mediates between the world and our natural human appetites for food, love, self-esteem, sexual gratification, intellectual stimulation, and companionship. Problems for many of us arise because the ego, while on a worthy mission, has no sense of proportion. It has a tendency to say things like, "You want a cookie? How about a whole box? Why stop at one glass of wine when you can drink every drop you can get your hands on?" Unleavened by our higher nature, ego lacks the moral and spiritual forces that add balance and proportion to our lives. Ego on its own will not acknowledge itself as part of the larger whole, which demands fairness, sharing, balance, harmony, and community.

The idea that the ego is a sinister part of us has been enhanced by many religions, which make self-annihilation the goal of spiritual growth and unfoldment. The path of self-annihilation may work for those who intend to live their lives sheltered from everyday realities, in the confines of ashrams or monasteries, but for the rest of us, nothing could be more impractical. We are trying to make our way in the material world and still be spiritual beings.

How can we accomplish this?

The answer is with an ego that exists in proportion to a healthy conscience. The first techniques I suggest to bring your ego into balance are visualization and dialogue. They help to reach a part of you that has been hidden from you for much of your life. While you have been out in the open and held accountable for your actions, your ego has been in hiding. Although your ego has been at the bottom of the things you've done, it has not been held accountable, because to everyone but you it is silent and invisible.

I encourage clients to conceptualize the ego not only as shadow but also as a twin self. The thoughts and actions of both you and your ego create all of your negative and positive qualities.

First close your eyes. See yourself opening your arms as you would to greet a friend. Now, embrace your ego, the mischief-maker who is stirring up all the trouble in your life. You may see your ego as all your defects and uncontrolled appetites rolled into one. After your embrace, step apart and ask ego to sit down. Just as if he were an actual person, talk with him. Let him know that you are not absolving yourself for your difficulties, and you need him to face your character defects with you.

The talk might go something like this:

You: "We're in a mess, you and I. What's going on?"

Ego: "I didn't get what I wanted. I wanted to do what I wanted to do when I wanted to do it. No controls. No limits. I encouraged you to eat and drink and buy what you wanted, go where you wanted, and not have to pay for a thing. I even showed you how to treat others so they would know who was boss. What's the problem?"

You: "The problem is obvious. Each person needs to live in balance and in sanity, so they can hear God's voice when He speaks. You're not mentioning how afraid I became because of you, not to mention the hundreds of shameful things we did together. Moving in the middle of the night to avoid creditors or always having to make new friends because we drove the ones we had away."

Ego: "I know you weren't happy with the way things were."

You: "First, we are going to believe it's possible to change. No situation is hopeless unless we adopt a pessimistic outlook or decide to become a permanent victim. Second, God will help us if we ask Him to. The universe is good and He is our source. We've been hoodwinking ourselves all our lives and now it is time to take our spirit back."

Ego: "What if I don't like living the way you are suggesting?"

You: "God will refund your misery."

Ego: "Him? How do you know He will want me back?"

You: "Ego, if He's taken me, he'll take you."

Ego: "I'm afraid that just saying His name will kill me."

You: "I'll help you. Let's start by spelling it. Here we go together."

You and Ego: "G-O-D. God."

This dialogue bears the hallmarks of a healthy conversation with the ego. First, it's friendly. We don't get anywhere by beating ourselves up. The process of transformation begins with self-acceptance. Second, it's effective. Some people believe it takes forever to get back into God's graces. However, it is amazing how quickly things begin to turn around when you feel that your ego and you are aligned in purpose. My clients have testified to this fact. One client recently commented, "I never had a clue that somebody with my checkered past could feel so free once I stopped blaming my ego and cleaned up my act."

Finally, this sample dialogue between self and ego is transformative. Once there is a true coming to terms with the ego, many people experience a breakthrough. Coming to honest terms with self is the first step in the spiritual experience, just as the caterpillar must spend time in a cocoon before becoming a butterfly. When you confront your ego, you can have a happier, freer life.

The ego is not our enemy. The ego is our strongest ally. But it must go through a psychic change. There is a powerful transcendence that happens when the ego confesses to how it has misled us.

When I was in college, the teachings of Carl Jung, a Swiss psychotherapist, rang true for me: he used astrology birth charts to diagnose a patient's difficulties. Jung refused to see a patient who would not let him use astrology to guide the therapy.

Jung's father was a minister in the Swiss Reformed Church, and several of his uncles were parsons. Very early in his life, Jung experienced dreams and visions of a religious nature, which convinced him that religion was a personal matter that had little to do with established creeds. He also was convinced that God had a "dark" side—which he later determined was man's ego—which did not accord with the conventional Christian image of an ever-loving father. Jung, therefore, found himself in the position of being unable to subscribe to the faith on which he had been reared, while at the same time continuing to think that individuals could be neither happy nor healthy unless they acknowledged their dependence upon some higher power rather than upon the ego.

The strongest argument Jung offered for the realized self was when he said that the collective unconscious part of us must awaken, become conscious, and that the ego must redeem the self by being individuated. Individuation can only happen when we turn away from the crowd and find our answers within ourselves when we cease to care what other people think of us and our behavior.

The ego can either be fed or faced. It is like you have a white dog and a black dog living within you. When you pray and meditate, see God in everyone, and live in truth, the white dog wins. When you live in darkness, blame others, and refuse to pray and meditate and change, the black dog prevails. Which one is winning within you? The one you're feeding!

What I know without doubt is that I have listened to my ego through many lifetimes with the same destructive results. One particular incident several years ago comes to mind that still causes me great pain.

It was the Christmas of 1978. I had returned to Birmingham for the holidays with my family, and my mother Maggie invited me to stay with her. Her apartment was attractive but small. Since I was a full-blown alcoholic, I should have stayed in a hotel.

On Christmas Eve I'd been on an all-day ho-ho holiday toot. The minute I walked through the door two hours late, my mother glared at me, hands on her hips.

"You ought to be ashamed of yourself, coming into my house drunk as a skunk. Some things never change. If you don't know how to respect me, stay away."

I had been at a college friend's house drinking from lunch until after six o'clock. I was expected home to take my mother to a party at my sister's. Couldn't mother understand that I was having a few drinks with a friend and his wife?

The ego struck the match and lit the fires of fear. I pulled out all the stops and leveled my 110-pound, five-foot-tall mother: "You are nothing but a goddamned bitch. I hate you. You have been a martyr since the day Daddy left you high and dry with six kids. I wish you were dead."

Mother had been dressing; she was putting on her good jewelry, most of which were gifts from me. She said not a word but instead turned and walked into her bedroom, and meticulously boxed everything I had ever given her. Maggie came back into the living room laden with tiny boxes.

"Here. Take this. I don't want any of it. I never want anything from you again as long as I live." As she left, she slammed the door, leaving me alone in my shame.

And Maggie, queen of hearts, the mother who had paid off loans and fielded hostile telephone calls from creditors, who had lain awake nights wondering if I would come home from a drunken all-nighter, and the biggest defender behind my back and detractor to my face, cried, and I heard her heart break.

The same little boy who won the spelling bee and poetry festival in grade school, made all A's in high school and had perfect attendance in Sunday school—a God-fearing, sweet-as-pie Southern gentleman—grew up to cut his mother to ribbons rather than face his own demons. It is the nature of a runaway ego, deadly as a king cobra and no respecter of persons, not even my own mother.

After I got sober in 1980, I made direct amends to my mother for all the lies I'd told, the bad loans she'd co-signed, the killing words I'd spoken, and the blame I'd laid at her feet. As Maggie lay dying in March 1996, I held her hand, kissed her wrinkled face, wept deep tears of sorrow and gratitude for having her as my mother, and watched her spirit leave her body. My clearing left time to heal what our respective karmas demanded we experience and forgive. We were two distinctly different people, but I came to love and adore her. The same thing happened with my absentee father. The day before he died I made amends with him. Both my parents were great teachers.

Are there souls who never make it back home? What happens to them? Many lost souls refuse to reform. They cling to remnants of the ego like a drowning man does to a life raft.

As a runaway child leaves home when he doesn't want to follow his parents' house rules, these souls reenter Earth's vibration and are drawn through the law of attraction to human beings who have become captive to addictions like alcohol, drugs, and sex and who wallow in anger, rage, and resentments.

Evil is an ego that has traveled many roads in many lifetimes without making proper corrections. When you die you return to an interdimensional world that is silent, invisible, and beyond the comprehension of humans.

I began to understand more clearly how the ego palmed off a life on man that man could not support. Man was never who the ego told him he was, and the day of reckoning would come sooner rather than later. I thought of the emperor's "clothing". We keep supporting something that does not exist.

After stirring awake, I headed for the pool at the top of the hill. The hot afternoon sun ruled in a blue sky with cotton-candy clouds. Some of the ego information bothers me, I mused as I swam. There has to be some piece of the puzzle I'm missing.

I got out of the pool and headed for my cottage. I talked to the committee in my head. "How can humanity be so dastardly? I asked out loud.

I am a formidable opponent to fairy-dust spirituality. I am stubborn and do not accept anything hook, line, and sinker; I question and I reason. Just as I positioned myself for a long, contemplative sit-down and talk-off, a child's voice spoke from the base of the boulder.

"Hello. My name is Angelo, but my granddaddy calls me Angel. What's your name?"

Startled, I jumped from the boulder and stood facing a young Italian boy with curly black hair and sky-blue eyes.

"My name is Albert. I am happy to meet an angel. How old are you, Angelo?"

"Six," he said as we shook hands.

"Well, young man, you must think I'm crazy, talking to myself and all," I said, hoping he'd been too busy playing to hear my jabbering.

"I don't think you're crazy at all, sir. My granddaddy says that nothing's worth saying if you don't run it by yourself first."

I was falling for those big blue eyes, and I was being lulled by his little-boy logic. Angelo was grinning at me like we both knew something.

"Thank God for granddaddy, Angelo. Do you always play by yourself?" I asked.

"Oh, I am never alone, Mr. Albert, but can I help you with your questions?"

I hoisted Angelo up onto the top of the rock and climbed up after him. He seemed pleased to be able to see the Pacific Ocean and the valley below. "Now, what do you know about egos and churches, young man?"

"Well, I don't know what da...dast...."

"Dastardly, Angelo, means cowardly," I offered.

"My granddaddy says that all of us can be good and all of us can be bad. We're not good all the time, but we're not bad all the time either. But, he says, 'Angel, if you don't look at what's bad, you'll never get good.'" Angelo said this in what must have been a good imitation of his granddaddy.

And in a moment, this child let me know that the universe was not always negative, but that man had to see what needed to be changed in order for his life to be better. I jumped from the rock and lowered Angelo to the safety of the ground. He gripped me tightly around my neck.

"I've got to go see a wise man about a riddle, Angelo. How long are you staying at the San Ysidro Ranch? Maybe I'll see you around later," I said as I started to leave.

"I'm not staying at the ranch. I'm staying..."

"...with granddaddy," we answered in unison and started laughing loudly and uncontrollably.

As Angelo looked into my eyes, he said, "I like to go to church because I see angels like me. They come in when the music starts, and leave when the minister starts to preach." Angelo grinned as he spoke.

"Before we say good-bye, Angelo, promise me that you'll never stop seeing angels and you'll keep listening to granddaddy."

We shook hands and I left.

As I hurried away from Angelo, he cried out to me, "Mr. Albert…"

I turned quickly and ran back toward the child, and then stopped suddenly. It was either the sun hitting the back of Angelo's head or one of those damn miracles, but I saw a large aura, a shaft of golden light, encase my little friend.

"Yes, Angelo, what is it?" I asked

"You're an angel, too," he said softly, and then ran higher into the mountains.

I ran all the way back to my cottage. Inside my room I looked into the face of profound sadness. Tears knocked out the dam that had held my emotions for more than fifty years. I loved the little boy in me—really loved him. And for the first time in my life I felt freer.

I soaked in a hot bath and ordered an in-room massage. When the masseur had finished kneading every sore spot in my body and gently activated all acupuncture points, I fell into bed and slept soundly. As I drifted off, a voice whispered, "And a child shall lead them."

Chapter 5

God or No God?

I woke up to the radio blaring "heavy traffic jams on Highway 101," "Dow Jones up 35 points," and "tension builds in the Middle East."

The phone rang.

"Drats," I mumbled, "no one knows I'm here."

"Ramapriya, this is Amrita, Swami Swahananda's secretary. Swami is going to be in Montecito at the Sarada Convent tonight. He wants you to have dinner with him."

"How are you, Amrita? Has your Aquarian mischief gotten you into any un-Vedanta-like situations lately? How do you know where I am?" I asked.

"I'm still making them crazy, Ramapriya. Your voice mail said that you were in Montecito. We know you stay at the San Ysidro Ranch."

Throughout the centuries, India has produced great teachers. One was Ramakrishna, the founder of Vedanta, who lived from 1836 to 1886. Ramakrishna is the chosen ideal for Vedantists, just as Jesus is for Christians. His brand of spirituality inspired a group of young disciples to form a monastic community.

Vedanta is a philosophy based on the teachings of the Vedas, ancient Hindu scriptures. Their basic instruction is that our true nature is divine. God, the Atman or Brahmin—the underlying reality—exists in each of us.

One of the deciding factors in my conversion from Christianity to Vedanta was *How to Know God: the Yoga Aphorisms of Patanjali*. Vedanta believes that all paths that lead to God are right paths. This philosophy complements my twelve-step program.

The Vedanta Society of Southern California was founded in 1929. It maintains a temple, convent, and monastery in Hollywood and Santa Barbara, and monasteries in Trabuco Canyon and San Diego.

I love invitations to eat at the Sarada Convent, because I am always a bit irreverent with its spiritual residents, who are called nuns. Before initiation, they are on probation for one year, and they take their final vows after ten years.

The nuns run a bookstore, where I shop as much for baubles as for books, which cover all religions of the world. There are nightly vespers and Sunday services in the temple perched amidst oleanders, cymbidia, and ceanothus, as well as olive and oak trees, Monterey pines, and eucalypti.

I met the nuns when a friend asked me to prepare and interpret astrology charts for them. As God-filled as these sweet peas are, life in a convent is not all Hallelujah Chorus. They struggle with God's will and sometimes fight among themselves. For more than ten years I have commissioned one of Montecito's best pastry chefs to bake a cake for each nun on her birthday. I get a lot of thank-you notes describing in delicious detail what kind of cake Christine Dahl made for them.

This holy place coexists with the *Architectural Digest*–perfect world of antique Louis tables and chairs, overpriced armoires, heavy drapes, and priceless rugs in Spanish-land-grant haciendas, Tuscan palazzi, and English manor houses. Vedanta teaches detachment. Old money and parvenus from Montecito, Santa Barbara, and Ojai flock to temple services at the Vedanta Temple.

When I was first initiated into Vedanta, I wanted everyone I knew to join. Many times the nuns quietly told me to stop proselytizing. In my early days as a devotee I was harsh about the wealthy, who appeared to prefer their fancy clothes and fine cars and houses to God. One of the nuns cautioned, "They'll either get it or they won't. It's not your business. It's God's business."

I was mobbed by the nuns when I arrived. They cajoled me to repeat jokes and tell every silly story I'd heard since my last meal at the harvest table. In the early days of "getting to know you" I smoked cigarettes (God forgive me), and the nuns dutifully provided an ashtray. It seems that a holy man from the order smoked. Tonight it was tea and coffee.

Right after dinner, Swami and I walked the back roads of this Eden in the mountains. As the sun set, mist rolled in from the ocean.

We did not speak for a long time.

Swami broke the silence. "Ramapriya, what does my birth chart say about my health? You can speak openly. I am a big boy."

I brought my guru's chart up on the screen of my mind. "Are you having any problems with either your gallbladder or liver, Swami? Are you considering surgery?" I asked.

"I am scheduled for gallbladder surgery at eight o'clock tomorrow morning," he answered.

"Why did you ask me about your health if you had already scheduled surgery?" I asked with surprise.

"I want to make sure astrology agrees with medicine," he said with a chuckle. "Why do you question your meditation when you do what meditation suggests?" he boomeranged.

"I was told that in 2012 there would be a consciousness shift and that I had to be prepared for it," I blurted out quickly.

"Ramapriya, stay in the present moment. The shift will take care of itself," my teacher counseled me.

I was not finished. I decided to push the river with my guru. "While in meditation I got information about how we need to change our lives through a set of lessons. Yesterday the lesson was the ego is not the enemy."

Swami motioned for me to sit with him beneath a large oak. He sat in a yoga posture and began to meditate. My teacher said as he drifted away, "The answers are where the questions are. Your ego gives you false answers to misleading questions."

And with that, Swami went quickly where he always goes when he meditates. Pulling my prayer chadar around my shoulders, I crossed my legs and shut my eyes.

Lesson 2:

God or No God?

When I was a child, I desperately wanted to know God. Church music and Bible stories excited me. I took lots of retreats to the mountains and the beach. One question unsettled me. I asked, "If there is a God, why did I have club feet?'

As long as I was coddled and fussed over by doctors and nurses at Duke Hospital, I didn't have any problems. When I went home to my family, two brothers, three sisters and bickering parents, the subconscious butterflies-and-bees brain chatter started: I want to go back to the hospital. I want my nurses and my doctors. I don't like my brothers and sisters or my parents.

As a little boy, I heard voices and I saw what others couldn't. I knew what others didn't. No one was there to listen to me or tell me that I could trust what I saw and what I knew. I had no mentor. It was like living in a parallel universe: I talked to invisible people but was misunderstood by people I could see. In the world outside, I used tricks of survival. I did what I was told to do, and I believed what I was told to believe. Rather than develop a personality that could tell the truth, I told everybody what they wanted to hear.

I was raised a Baptist. Nonbelievers went to hell. I was baptized, but I never believed. I became a ministerial student and was a pastor in rural South Alabama churches, but I did not believe in Jesus as my Lord and Savior, and I did not believe that Jesus could get me in or keep me out of Heaven. The big buzz as a kid was "Have you accepted our Lord and Savior, Jesus Christ?" I said I had, but I hadn't. The still, small voice said, "Save yourself." But this was my secret. I never told anyone that I didn't believe. Who would I tell? Why would I risk rejection? Alcohol eventually helped me become defiant enough to excommunicate myself from traditional religion.

Spotting my struggle about Jesus, my guru gave me a mantra which included repeating the name Jesus over and over again. He later told me that it was his way of reuniting me with one of the world's greatest master teachers, Jesus Christ. Today, I use Christ's teachings as truths to edify my soul.

I dubbed myself President of the debate society. "If there is a God why is there so much poverty in the world? If God so loves us, why does he allow wars to go on and on and on? And why do innocent babies die at birth?" After booze rescued me from the hell of religiosity I was stuck in a black hole railing at injustices and shaking my fist at the Creator.

I was a stranger in a strange land.

God was never alive in my life until I found Him out of desperation when I got sober. Some man in the rooms of sobriety told me that he used a doorknob as his Higher Power. A doorknob as God would never have worked for me. I needed the big guy in the sky or wherever He was, and nothing else would do for me.

I prayed and meditated before and after I sobered up. In a moment of clarity during prayer and meditation, I intuited that God loved me. I felt He cared for me, and He "said" if I worked a few steps my life would get better. I did the steps, and my life got a lot better—better than any screenwriter could conjure up.

My relationship with God involved obedience. Paul told me that I had fallen from grace, that in the past I had found the name of God repugnant. In past lives I had served the God of the church and had no personal relationship with the divine Creator. Returning to God was like a child learning his ABC's or how to ride a bicycle. My return to God meant that I had to become teachable again and to do things that were uncomfortable to me. I had to make time for God, and I had to listen to Him through the still, small voice of intuition. The power of the ego was still rampant, but each day I did what I was told. With the help of the God within me, I exercised right use of will. My life changed profoundly. My life gets better every day when I use the tools I have been given.

When I was in my 20s, I read *Many Mansions* by Dr. Gina Cerminara, based on the case studies of sleeping-prophet psychic Edgar Cayce, dubbed so because he would diagnose illnesses while in a deep trance. Cayce fascinated me because he had been born a traditional Christian. So had I. We had the same birth chart, different years: Leo rising, Taurus Moon, and the Sun in Pisces.

A major stumbling block for me was that if God was all-seeing and all-knowing, He would know that I had done too many bad things to accept me back into the fold. *Many Mansions* agreed with me. We must seek forgiveness—make amends—for the harm we have done ourselves and others. We cannot see or hear God through static interference, which is what our errant ways become.

Many Mansions said that we must face what we have inflicted on someone else. If we don't settle the score at the time, we will reincarnate and have to feel what we have done to another in a subsequent life.

Toward the end of her life, I met Dr. Cerminara after writing her a fan letter. She called me on the telephone, and when I asked her why she would call me when she didn't know me, she said: "Have you ever gotten one of your letters?" She had moved to Ojai, in a subdivision run by the Theosophical Society, whose most famous teacher was Krishnamurti. She invited me to visit her. I drove up one Sunday morning very early and stayed until 3 o'clock in the morning. It was one of the most interesting days of my life.

When I asked Gina whether or not I had actually been a centurion, she said that if I were very clear and open to past lives, I would be inspired in meditation with honest and objective answers. She said that as time passed, there would be many confirmations of whether I had or had not been.

She was right. I have come to know that I had club feet because I broke the feet of convicted criminals around the time of Christ. My intuition seemed to say to me, "You want to know how painful your acts were? Here are the feet to remind you." My club feet were also a reminder to stand on my own two feet.

I have learned why a lot of things happened in former lives and in this one. But I have had the greatest difficulty in knowing who God is and what He expects of me. I have had the same trouble with God that all mankind has had, because we look for him in the same way: We try to figure out who God is, instead of allowing him to reveal himself. *How to Know God* teaches that universal God is known as Brahman and that man can reach the God within, the Atman, through concentration and meditation.

Here are some things I did to find God: A meditation teacher led me to get quiet and to listen to the God within me. I began the practice of yoga—the spiritual discipline and techniques of meditation that enabled me to achieve knowledge of God. I disciplined myself to quietude every day at a set time. God touched me and he opened my heart. My sneaky mind eventually gave way to tranquil contemplation.

The longer you pray and meditate, the more quickly God will speak to you and the sooner you will live with inspiration and courage instead of fear.

I often look everywhere outside myself for solutions. God is within, just as the ego is a part of me. God is the creator of all, including the ego. The role of the God within is to love and guide us when we will allow it.

God is permissive and will allow us to make poor choices and unwise decisions—to be as errant and mischievous as we want to be. However, we will pay the price by being isolated and separated from God: If we drink too much, we go to jail; couple indiscriminately, get the disease; judge another, we're convicted. God has not wreaked havoc on us. We create our own reality.

God will wait patiently for us to get sick and tired of bad-boy and bad-girl behavior. When we turn everything over to God, our lives will be worth living. Ego tries to divide, separate, and deceive us with self-importance, while God says that we are all His precious children.

Many people view Him as a punishing God. If we are not good, if we break the Ten Commandments, if we commit adultery, we will suffer. Churches use fear and intimidation as a way to bring the errant ones back into line with existing church tenets and beliefs.

I see God as a clown, laughing at how seriously we take ourselves. We make plans, He rearranges. Power brokers roll the dice for world dominance. God gets a kick out of how we think we are in control.

When I was initiated into the Vedanta Society, some of my friends asked why I would join a religion when I believe in nothing—I know what I know by experience. I repeat what got me to join: "All paths that lead to God are right paths."

The *Bhagavad Gita* reminds us that the war is always within. If you want to see who the enemy is, look inside. If you want to know who is out to get you, look in the mirror. If ego and God are within, that's where the war that can be won is being waged.

The gist of the *Bhagavad Gita* is that when you take the struggle inside and deal with your own devils, when you see that you are your enemy, the sabers cease to rattle, and you are left with peace.

God is love, and He allows you to live the life you are willing to pay the price to create. God is constant and eternal. Love does not need to defend and deny. It is the divided ego that maneuvers to keep man in confusion.

God or No God? For me, there is no question that God is within me and without him I would be absolutely nothing.

I stirred back to consciousness as tiny beads of rain dripped from the jacarandas. Swami stood over me.

"Ramapriya, I do not know if you talk in your sleep, but you mumble in meditation. Practice shutting down the mind, and soon the chatter will cease as well."

I wasn't finished yet with my opportunity to plumb Swami's reservoir of knowing on the way back to the Sarada Convent. "Why do I have trouble with unconditional love?"

"If God and ego are the same, and if both live inside of you, let God speak more and let the ego listen. Perhaps you need a silent weekend, Ramapriya."

Again we walked without words, and I felt God beginning to lull my ego to sleep.

Chapter 6

The Light and the Family

Travel through Upper and Lower Egypt is tough. As tour escort, I am responsible for twelve travelers getting out of bed at the crack of dawn, eating breakfast, being on time at designated pickup points, and getting in and out of museums and monuments. Feeding them is akin to trying to get ten year-olds to table: "Albert, can't we see one more tomb before we eat?"

This group had two pluses that made the trip manageable: Our number was small, and we had a knowledgeable Egyptologist. There were an equal number of men and women, who were as convivial when we started as they were when we got back.

If you go to the land of the Nile between November and May, the weather is cooler. Reflecting sand is deadly hot, even when temperatures are moderate. So many tombs are underground, and heat variance of a few degrees makes a difference.

A typical sight is hordes of drifting sightseers with cameras flung about their necks, passports and Egyptian pounds hidden beneath their clothing, clutching large bottles of mineral water. Throngs of beggars and hawkers thrust their wares at captive travelers, from fake glass beads and crinkled postcards to plaster busts of pharaohs and the ever-peripatetic tee shirts.

Egypt and Sedona share a similar frequency. I was eager to know what I would see and hear in Abu Simbel, the monument to Ramses II; at the Valley of the Kings and Queens, particularly the shrine dedicated to the only woman ever to rule Egypt, Hatshepsut; during the light shows in the temples of Luxor and Karnak; and visiting again the many ancient digs, tombs, museums, and antiquities. Coming back to Egypt so soon after the Harmonic Convergence, made me more aware that I might feel Isis's power more strongly than that of Osiris.

A lot of people tour Egypt looking for the "aha" that so many books about this ancient land promise. There are tour guides who insinuate that a traveler just might feel the presence of spirit, like Napoleon Bonaparte reportedly did when he slept in the Great Pyramid; or be given a profound omen when the world will end and how; or perhaps channel Cleopatra. Some are encouraged to solve a mystery beneath the ground in an excavated burial site like King Tutankhamen's tomb. I always tell my groups to expect the unexpected but I am talking more about the hardships of traveling in a third world country or getting use to a diet to which they are unaccustomed or hordes of children crying, "Baksheesh, baksheesh." When you go to Egypt go without expectations. See and feel and absorb what is in this strange but beckoning vortex of spiritual beauty filtered through toxic haze.

Our groups meditate to synthesize our energies to ancient events and thought impressions, or sit in a cool spot in a temple and discuss the mythology of this sacred spot. Like Sedona, Egypt will bring your stuff up and force you to face unresolved issues. On one of my journeys to Cairo, Luxor and Aswan I had to mediate an ego war between two guests who both thought they were the reincarnation of Hatshepsut. I settled the score when I said I thought they had both been her servants. They fumed, but we cleared the air. All who go to Egypt have the best time if they bring their well-mannered inner child along. I remember to pack a healthy sense of humor before I leave home.

What I pray happens to each of us—rather than the razzle-dazzle of spiritual transformation—is that we open ourselves to the melodies of the setting sun and the resurgence at day break of the adventures that can lead to psychic change—to rediscover the forgotten true self. Before we leave the sand and sounds of Aton Ra and Ramses, I wish for everyone to find a deep and abiding peace that echoes through the Valley of the Kings and Queens.

We stayed at the Mena House, a royal hunting lodge built for Khedive Isma'il and converted into a guest house in time for the opening of the Suez Canal in 1869. The main hotel is situated just below the Great Pyramid of Cheops and surrounded by beautiful gardens. Mosquitoes and flies were the only insults to the harmony of this grand hotel.

Most of the travelers were younger than I, so they danced at the nightclubs into the wee hours, yet sprang into the tour buses every morning. They had waited all their lives to come to this land of mythological mischief, so they were not going to waste time sleeping.

Before retiring the first night, I sat on my balcony facing the Great Pyramid. The centuries-old monument seemed close enough to touch. It is the largest of three pyramids located within a few hundred yards of one another.

Memories of my first trip to Egypt are vivid, for it was a wild roller-coaster ride when Patrick Flanagan, author of *Pyramid Power*, and his beautiful wife Gael brought me here as their guest. In a psychic trance, his spirit guide, Master K, spoke through and said that the Flanagans were to bring me *back* to Egypt, where I had lived many times. (Although I came to question channeling, I was happy to be going to Egypt.) The Egyptians revere Patrick as they would a god. The tour company with whom he had worked for years picked us up in an air-conditioned Mercedes Benz, booked us into five-star hotels, and reserved a five-night Nile cruise on the best boat in Egypt.

A woman from Oklahoma named Lavendar, who considers herself a white witch, had invited a number of guests, including the Flanagans and me, to gather in Cairo for the Pleiadian Alignment on November 17th, 18th, and 19th. The prerequisite was that each traveler have a personal planet—Sun, Moon, Mercury, Venus, Mars, or Saturn—at the 26th degree of any astrological sign. Lavendar was convinced that people with this configuration had a special destiny in the whatever-was-to-come world. My Mars is at that degree, conjunct the mid-heaven of my chart. Lavendar went wild when she heard this. Shirley MacLaine, who jolted the collective consciousness with her best-seller, *Out on a Limb,* was in the group as well.

I reflected on my initiation in the King's Chamber during the Pleiadian Alignment. Certain adherents of esoteric astrology believed that spirit overlords from the outer limits would release special alchemical energy along a twenty-six degree angulation onto us pilgrims holding an all-night vigil in the Great Pyramid. We would be telepathically hooked up to a mother lode of insights about quantum physics that would reveal our true identity, and we would be given our mission on Earth. I hadn't a clue what any of it meant at the time and still don't. "Let it be revealed in God's time," the voice of intuition said to me. Thank God today I believe that I am just an ordinary man living an extraordinary life.

Shirley MacLaine went on a private trek down the River Nile with a special Egyptologist. She had her own personal initiation inside the sarcophagus of the King's Chamber of the Great Pyramid with no one present but Lavendar.

I had a typical spicy Egyptian dinner with Shirley and the Flanagans in a tent with rugs on the ground the night before our initiations. Those were my cigarette-smoking days, so when the party got rowdy, Shirley bummed Kools from me and we puffed away as she held court. Shirley is no nonsense, and she speaks her mind and states her truth. The repartee between her and Patrick turned out to be anything but cordial. Accusations from Shirley about inappropriate behavior atop the Great Pyramid of Cheops by a group that Patrick had brought to Egypt the year before made Flanagan furious. The dinner ended abruptly with bruised feelings and name calling. There were no Southern manners that night.

What I will never forget about my alone time with Shirley, if I live to be a hundred and one, is that she and I are soul mates, a spiritual brother and sister. She was then what I was to become: direct, oftentimes confrontational and she stands by what she knows, even if everybody else in the room disagrees with her. Shirley is like Henry Fonda in the movie *Twelve Angry Men:* she can get you to switch your vote to her point of view. And years later we shared a synchronicity: Simon & Schuster published her book *The Camino: a Journey of the Spirit* at the same time they published mine, *Signs and Wonders, Understanding the Language of God.* Known as the Camino, Santiago de Campostela is a famous pilgrimage that has been undertaken by people for centuries across northern Spain. Paulo Coelho, whose quote appears on this book's cover and who gave me a quote for *Signs and Wonders,* wrote *The Alchemist,* his international best seller while on a pilgrimage like the one MacLaine took. I consider my connection to Shirley a foreshadowing of my Coelho connection.

This trip was a harbinger of things to come for her. Having felt as if her career had fallen through the floor, she went on her own Grail quest all over the world, looking for answers to who she was and what God wanted her to do with her life. She felt that her Creator wanted her to tour the country to teach people what she knew, and how each of them could enrich their lives with the tools she gave them. In two years she spoke to thousands of people all over the United States. She charged three hundred dollars per person: a hundred dollars for the body, a hundred dollars for the mind and a hundred dollars for the soul.

MacLaine, known as much for her blithely unconventional persona (and her New Age beliefs) as she is for a career that has spanned theatre, film and television, won an Emmy for *Gypsy in My Soul* and an Oscar for *Terms of Endearment.* Her books, starting with *Out on a Limb,* have all been international best sellers. All of this happened after Shirley's initiation in the Great Pyramid under the Pleiadian alignment. Now that's getting a power jolt from the great beyond.

During my turn in the tomb, Lavendar placed coded crystals at each of my chakras. Hovering over me, she chanted and waved a purple crystal wand from a small pedestal at the head of the crypt. While in a deep meditation, I saw myself in France and heard the name "Toulouse" repeated over and over. I felt a shiver chill, and a current of electricity radiated from my head to my feet.

Another Albert, perhaps the real me, was synchronistically coming into being not only through an initiation inside the Great Pyramid but also astrologically it was time to let go of the people-pleasing, accommodating person I had always been. With this cognition came an overwhelming desire to leave these people and get away from their rituals.

A few years later I would go on another spiritual quest, from Toulouse, France across the Pyrenees and into Aix-en-Provence near Marseille, ending on the French Riviera. It was as if a childhood scripture spoke to my illumined soul: *"For now we see in a mirror, darkly; but then face to face: now I know in part, but shall I know fully even as also I was fully known."* The Grail Quest through France was softer, quieter and there were prisms of light, subtle but transforming. France was more like traveling with my authentic self, to see what I could see with new eyes and hear with new ears. Nothing similar to the initiation in the Great Pyramid would happen to me until Paul revealed himself in Birmingham a few years later.

After our two-week adventure in Upper and Lower Egypt, the Flanagans took me to Greece for three days to relax and assimilate all that we had experienced. Patrick, never too generous with a compliment, said, "Albert, you got your power back."

Buzzing and biting mosquitoes brought me back to the present. I went inside and slept deeply and peacefully. We had a lot of places to visit, and my eager beavers would be up early.

The first two days of the trip we knelt and prayed in several mosques, touched the sphinx and studied its paws which some believed contained the hall of records. Several in our group meditated, trying to pick up vibrations about these documents that chronicle not only how the Sphinx was built but also the Great Pyramid. We were dazzled by all the sarcophagi and precious jewels and trinkets in the display cases of the Egyptian Antiquities Museum, especially the famous King Tutankhamen artifacts. The Sound and Light Performance at the Pyramids of Giza both educated and entertained us. Yet because of the heat, the ever-present crowds, and the need to start early every day to go to the tombs and monuments, the land of the pharaohs is still exhausting ... and the tour schedule a grind.

We shopped for scarabs, the dung beetles made from lapis and other less-expensive stone materials, fabrics, perfumes, spices and gold and silver jewelry at Khan el Khalili bazaar, where the sideshow of people is mesmerizing. The scarab represents death and rebirth in Egyptian mythology. Our group bargained lower prices for personalized cartouches for us and our friends back home. We bought tailor-made long, flowing galabiyas, caftans worn throughout Egypt by men and women.

The fourth morning, our cruise boat docked in Luxor. We walked a mile with our guide to Dendera, a temple dedicated to Hathor, goddess of love and fertility. Legend claims that Hathor and Isis, mother goddess of Egyptian mythology, are aspects of the same deity. Osiris and Isis are considered the father and mother god in the polytheistic ancient Egyptian religion.

Dendera is in alignment with another ancient temple near Luxor, at Edfu, dedicated to Horus, consort of Hathor. Completing this Egyptian triangle is a temple called Abydos, built to honor Seti I. All monuments, temples, and burial grounds have suffered major deterioration from weather and little upkeep and desecration by Coptic Christians. Dendera conjured up powerful memories for the entire entourage. Although our group included an architect, a designer, a teacher, and several trust-fund babies, none in the group was a "twinky"—a word coined by my friend Beirne in Sedona to refer to someone who will believe anything, with little discernment in spiritual matters.

I wandered off by myself into some of Dendera's many chambers and small anterooms that were once altars of worship. I followed a shaft of light that I spotted across the width of the temple, which poured in through a small rooftop chasm created when a large column had fallen from its holding. The sun's rays splayed, causing shadows from the supports to cascade in domino fashion.

I sat on a small marble bench and rested my head against a support. I closed my eyes as my breathing became even and still. I relaxed in a slow-descending elevator that took me to a well-known place in the theatres of my mind.

Lesson 3:

The Light Will Never Fail

"In the beginning God created the Heavens and the Earth. And the Earth was without form, and void; and darkness was upon the face of the deep. And the Spirit of God moved upon the face of the waters. And God said, Let there be light: and there was light." —Genesis 1:1–3.

I was back in Egypt to face both my dark side and the light that is within me. Both were created by God. When man refused the light, darkness was created. As God and the ego are one and within me, so are light and dark, day and night parts of divine creation.

Carl Jung wrote in *The Essential Jung* that God has a dark side, which is the macrocosmic ego. The devil sought to set up a kingdom of his own by trying to convince man that there was no God. In the mid-twentieth century, philosopher Nietzsche stated that God was dead. Jung rediscovered God as a guiding principle of unity within the depths of the individual psyche.

God in his mercy created darkness so that man could work out those evil parts of himself that keep him alienated from the Creator. In the absence of light we can feel the cellular pain of being the un-self—a runaway and errant lost child.

God is light and God is love. The low-self ego nature is dark and incapable of love. Much like a narcissist, the ego is self-absorbed, selfish, self-centered, and it receives for the self alone. It creates the chaos in our lives.

The light of God is the divine spark that was in us at birth. The divine spark is our eternal cord connection to the One Living God. It is who we are at our deepest core, and it is what we have yet to become. It is our promise that all things are possible if we rekindle the light. Why, then, do we not manifest this incredible beingness of light on Earth? Why are we not at peace, and what is darkness?

We are not at peace because cellular memory stirs us to dim the light; we are not as we were created, and we are not living with what binds us to our true essence of unconditional love.

Darkness is God's gift to us. Light can only be revealed from darkness. It is God's permissiveness that lets us turn away from his love and live in the kingdom of desire and darkness. As a parent needs for his child to learn from disobedience, God permits us to come out of darkness and into the light, enveloped in His grace.

When I was getting sober, a handsome Navy lieutenant whom I will call Laurence used to lead a lot of twelve-step meetings, and he was so silly that one day I reproached him, "Laurence, alcoholism is a deadly disease, and all you do is act silly from the podium. Stop joking around. Take recovery more seriously."

"Albert," Laurence said, "we drunks have cried over the rotten things we've done long enough—we have lived in the dark night of the soul. When we sobered up we insisted on enjoying life. Lighten up. The next time I see you, make me laugh." He grinned at me then walked away. I had a stunned look on my face. But I eventually learned to laugh at myself before anybody else did. When I learned to laugh, I did lighten up, and more of God's light shone through.

Light comes into us through the power of laughter.

God never leaves us. The light never extinguishes. If God is in us and a part of us, redemption will always be possible. As God is, so are we. We are who we are, even though from time to time we act contrary to our true nature.

Kabbalah teaches that man felt that he did not deserve the light of the Creator and that to continue to receive it without merit was creating "bread of shame," which is an undeserved reward. Man felt that in order to receive the light, he had to earn it. And in order to do so, he had to move from the chaotic limitations of what Kabbalah refers to as "the 1% world" and tap into "the 99% world"—which can only be accessed through his sixth sense. This ultimately will lead man to all possibilities and to receiving the Creator's light to share, rather than for the self alone. Man had to look in all the occult hideouts of evil and illumine his blackened soul.

As soon as I walked into the doors of recovery, a carpenter asked me to coffee after the meeting. When I laid out all my schemes for beating the drunk-driving charges—how I intended to go to meetings to make myself look good in court—the carpenter said to me, "Albert, it's not the court system that concerns us. We love you. And we are going to love you until you learn to love yourself." And they all did. Today, I love the newcomer to recovery.

Light comes into us through love.

Since my first trip to Egypt, my light had grown stronger, and I became aware that the direction of my life would alchemically change into one of greater purpose. The aim of the present journey was to wipe clean false perceptions about God and to embrace light by embracing and illuminating the dark. Converting the ego through love is the first step of redemption.

I was there in the light in the temple of Dendera for my own clearing. We cannot clear others until we come clean ourselves. I was learning that my ideas of dark and light had been contrary to natural law.

Darkness is an energy that separates us from God and from love. Darkness tells us that our feelings are real, but that God is not. Darkness tells us that only what we see, feel, touch, and smell are real and that everything else is an illusion. The opposite is true. Where light is absent, mind perversions and unnatural desires arise. The voice of darkness fuels negativity that we experience as hopelessness, fear, anger, envy, and mistrust. Darkness is where man goes to experience the cries and demands of his ego. On a deeper psychological level, the dark represents a reflection of man's thoughts and deeds committed in the absence of God. Darkness is godlessness.

Darkness is where evil lives, which is not only universal but it is a part of each of us. Kabbalah suggests that "the ultimate objective of spirituality is not to remove humanity's negative traits or even the existence of evil, but to confront and transform the dark forces within ourselves. It is this struggle that ignites the divine within each of us, allowing us to soar."

Without darkness there can be no light. Without the choice between good and evil, right and wrong, there can be no right use of will, and no decision to return to God. Light is who we are, and dark is not. We have assumed a nature that is not who we are. Light is our birthright, and it is to light that we will ultimately return.

In Javier Sierra's novel, *The Secret Supper*—in which the Holy Grail and eucharistic bread are missing and the apostles are well-known heretics in Leonardo da Vinci's painting *The Last Supper*—he solves historical mysteries based on real documentation and extensive field research.

Sierra writes about one of da Vinci's precepts regarding light: "Light is God's only resting place. God the Father is light, the heavens are light, everything, down deep, is light. That is why da Vinci kept repeating that if man succeeded in mastering light, he'd be able to summon forth God and speak to Him whenever he needed to."

What is more, Leonardo da Vinci believed that painters used light and dark tones to reveal messages: *"to those that hath eyes let them see."* This was the secret knowledge called the Art of Memory. Sierra writes, "da Vinci was sending light into the darkness.

God understands man's character. Created in his image, man is not God, but God is in man. Darkness is separation from God. Light is a power source of union and harmony and peace. It cannot judge, because it operates without prejudice, manipulation, arrogance, or need to control. Light is. Darkness is not.

Within each of us is the light. No matter what we do, how often we flee into darkness, light always is. When we are honest with ourselves about things that drive us into darkness—drunkenness, drugs, infidelities, lying, stealing, coveting, envying—we become enlightened, "in the light."

The void that the absence of God leaves is filled with diversions that prevent us from being who we are. Hence, we move toward darkness and away from the light.

Man can return to the light at any time. No authorities, deacons, elders, or character critics can keep man from the light, because the light always is and always will be within man. Light is man's birthright.

From time to time, prophets and teachers come to Earth to guide the fallen back to God. These leaders are venerated and worshiped. Their light is bright, and their magnetism draws the prodigal. Buddha, Krishna, Jesus, the Dalai Lama, and many others hold the light and use its essence to draw others to God. Their disciples proliferate year after year to perpetuate the teachings for all mankind.

The light will never fail. It was in the beginning and always will be within each of us. When we choose the path of darkness, the light weakens, but the electrical generator beams on. When the pain of separation is severe enough, the prodigal can return to the principle of creation.

The plan of Creation provides a road back to the light, a road back to redemption. It is the road back to who we really are—children of the light and children of God. To be redeemed by light is to become it. We become it by allowing it to work within us. When this happens, the darkness becomes dissolved in the light of our conscious awareness.

Gautama Buddha's most significant contribution to the spiritual life of humankind was to insist to his disciples, "Be a light unto yourselves." Ultimately, each of us must make our way through the darkness without any companions, maps, or guides.

As quickly as I moved into meditative mode, I came back to alert consciousness with someone pulling on my arm. It was a member of our tour group. "Albert, we've been looking everywhere for you. Did you forget that you're having high tea at three o'clock with a mystery lady on the boat?" Our travel director said that there was a surprise voyager from a separate tour group and he had arranged for her and me to meet alone on deck for high tea.

"I was not asleep, I was meditating. Yes, I remember my tea date with a woman I do not know," I replied.

"I distinctly heard you talking to someone, but there is no one here but you," she said.

Egypt inspires me and opens me up to all possibilities, especially with the Egyptians we meet along the way. Her people are precious to me. They are kind and loving toward us Americans. When the children beg for baksheesh, I want to take them home and give them a good education, clean clothes, and better sanitation. This is their country. This is their world. This is their karma. Who am I to interfere?

We arrived back at the boat in time for a delicious lunch. Nile cruise boats have the best food in Egypt, prepared by a top-notch chef, and everything is safe to eat.

I lay down for a quick nap before my tea date. Once more, I drifted immediately to that reservoir of information where truth lies. And once again I heard the powerful message: The light will never fail.

I lay still for a moment to process the information I had accessed. As Paul promised earlier, the mention of the word light made me feel more centered, more hopeful, and more connected to a power greater than me. I sat up to get ready for my rendezvous feeling weightless, and I could feel a peaceful inner center.

As I walked toward the open door to the terrace, shaded by a green-and-white-striped canopy with matching cushioned deck chairs and tiny café tables, I saw her seated in profile wearing those famous smoked eyeglasses. She was dressed in a beige twill suit with a black-patterned Hermes scarf around her shoulders. Madame wore little jewelry.

The wind was up and carried a light spray from the river. The boat moved slowly toward the heart of Luxor, where the cruise would end for her.

I crept quietly toward her. I suspected she was catnapping.

"Madame Sadat, I am Albert Gaulden," I stated rather formally.

"Oh, sorry, you gave me a start," Jehan Sadat said. "Please, sit here."

She motioned me to a chair to her right. I turned it slightly so I could see her better.

"Your tour operator tells me that you talk a lot about my husband, Anwar," she said with the trace of a smile.

"I speak of him often because no one has ever touched me like he did. When he died, I grieved as one would for his father. I call him Egypt's brightest light."

Madame Sadat sat quietly and stared into my eyes. A long time passed before either of us spoke.

On October 6, 1981, President Anwar el-Sadat was assassinated as he watched a military review celebrating the reclamation of lands from Israel. I was staying at the Regency Hotel in New York in 1978 when he, Menachem Begin, and President Jimmy Carter got off the elevator. They had been drafting peace accords. Sadat's piercing gaze into my eyes was like a lightning bolt to my nervous system.

That year I wrote a screenplay, *The World Is Waiting*, which ends in a peace festival in Cairo. A producer-partner arranged for us to meet with President Sadat in November 1981 to discuss filming in Egypt. He died the month before.

Jehan Sedat changed how we view women in the Arab world in her book *A Woman of Egypt*.

"Anwar was for all people. He believed more than anyone in peace in the Middle East," Madame Sadat said quietly.

Paul's voice played in my head:

Man loves darkness rather than light.

A butler poured tea, and we drank and talked for more than an hour. I told her about seeing her husband in New York with Begin and Carter, and about the meeting for my movie that was not to be.

"What incredible coincidences. What are the odds that you and I would meet?" she asked.

"There are no coincidences, Madame Sadat. Every thing in life is pre-planned," I said.

"Albert, who are you? What do you know and how do you know it?" she asked.

"Madame Sadat, I don't know how to answer that question. Peculiar things have been happening to me lately to change my perception of me and the world. This I do know: none of us is who we think we are, and things are not what they seem," I said.

We stared at the feluccas drifting by and waved to the workers tending their sails. Madame Sadat seemed to be processing what I had said.

"Tell me more about coincidences. They puzzle me," she said. Madame Sadat leaned in very close to my face and asked, "Do you think that Anwar's death was a struggle between good and evil or simply God's plan?" she asked.

I cleared my throat and paused to collect my thoughts. I knew that she knew the answer, but I still needed to measure my words.

I took both her hands and held them for a moment and then said, "You asked me two things. As far as coincidences are concerned, there are no coincidences and there are no accidents, including our meeting this afternoon. Everything we do and everything that happens to us, including the bad stuff, is by divine design; everything is pre-planned, albeit we have free will. My intuition tells me that the death of President Sadat was both a struggle between the dark side and God's will. President Sadat's death was karmic."

She closed her eyes and sat in the reflection of the setting sun. A sudden chill caused her to pull the oversized scarf more tightly around her shoulders.

"Why do you come here so often? What so fascinates you with this country," she asked.

"Sedona, Arizona, where I live, and Egypt are similar. As I watch the landscape along the Nile, I am reminded of Sedona. Sedona is known as Red Rock Country, because she is nestled in a valley of craggy reddish-brown sandstone formations millions of years old. If you look closely, hundreds of etched figures appear to stand guard over this rustic hamlet. I see the same faces in the mountains of sand and limestone here in Egypt.

"Legend contends that Sedona has eight or more whirling energy centers called vortexes which are either magnetic, electric, or electro-magnetic. When you are in one of these energy force fields, some people feel calmness, while others experience a sense of becoming unnerved. There are reports of hikers having a physical or emotional healing in these powerful eddies. Others say they have been spiritually transformed. Those who monitor lay-line grids, which are conduits for energy underground, as I do birth charts, or life roadmaps, say that heightened reception occurs in these places.

"Hopi elders say that we are ancestors of Egypt. Egypt draws me here, just as Sedona lures travelers to meditate and feel her transcendent vortexes. Your people are my people and my people are your people. We gather along the mystical Nile for reunion," I said.

I learned more about my adopted country from one who knew it well. Madame Sadat smiled when I spoke of Egypt's children and women and how both must be better schooled and protected.

"I feel as you do, Albert. The Egyptian woman is oppressed. The women here need better education and opportunities to become whatever their knowledge permits. Egypt in many ways still lives in the dark ages," she said.

As I started to leave, she grabbed my hand and held it for a moment. "Thank you for speaking to me about Anwar. I always like to hear how people everywhere love him."

"I hope that you do not think me presumptuous, but I feel that you and President Sadat are twin flames. You both hold a strong light for others. When I look at you, I see him. You are the same. His light, your light, will never fail."

She nodded with closed eyes.

Madame Sadat wanted to meet the rest of my group. She had seen us celebrating the birthday of one of our travelers in the dining room. The creative gifts given by my group to the celebrant were bought at the bazaars and from the hawkers at the monuments and tombs. Madame Sadat was fascinated by the ingenuity of our group.

I stood to leave. My group was peeking around the door from the lounge. I motioned to them, and like children excited and thrilled to be meeting such a famous lady, they came out quickly and I introduced each one.

As we left, I turned back and said, "Madame Sadat, Anwar did not die. He lives. I feel him, I see him with us now. He will affect the world for a long, long time. Thank you for courage to speak as you do here and in America and all over the planet about what needs to change in Egypt and the world."

Jehan Sadat smiled and nodded. Then she turned her head back toward the land we were leaving. I knew she wanted to be alone, and I left.

My sweet peas were bubbling over when we reconvened in the lower lobby. Each person saw Madame Sadat in his or her own way.

I recalled those famous lines from the *Rubáiyát of Omar Khayyám* as I stood on the deck of the boat. The good times and the tragedies in the life of President Anwar and Madame Jehan Sadat replayed in the theaters of my mind:

> The Moving Finger writes; and, having writ,
> Moves on: nor all thy Piety nor Wit
> Shall lure it back to cancel half a line,
> Nor all thy Tears wash out a word of it.

Feluccas dotted the Nile. They shuffled day workers from hotels and cruise boats. Voices amplified by megaphones cried out Islamic prayers, and the devout bowed and prayed in the direction of Mecca.

Dusk in Egypt is an eerie but magical tableau pictured time and again in travel magazines. Sounds and smells and swirling dust conjure memories of dynasties and deities who once ruled this strange and mystical sandbox.

Darkness crept over the horizon, but I could see the faint outline of Madame Sadat as she climbed the limestone steps to the boulevard above. At street level she looked toward the boat, and I waved. Jehan Sadat stepped into a car, and was gone.

I sat on the boat alone for most of the night. Around two o'clock in the morning I grabbed a couple of blankets from a stack on a nearby table. I was drifting, floating, sleeping, and dreaming. Paul soon came to tuck me in and hold me in God's grace as he repeated "the light will never fail."

At breakfast the next morning, the captain asked me to take a walk with him. We stopped at door 201. He opened it and we entered a suite with a sweeping view of the countryside disappearing behind the boat in muted blues, purples, and greens.

"This is Madame Sadat's suite. She designed this room. You are standing on an antique rug that has been in her family for centuries. This is her furniture, her antiques and tapestries. She asked that you stay here until you leave the boat in three days. If you need anything, please call me personally. Madame Sadat said for us to care for you as we do her," the captain said. He handed me the key.

I sat down dumbstruck. I am in her suite, I said to myself. This was over the rainbow. The bedroom was large enough to accommodate a king-sized bed with an antique gold-inlay headboard. I pulled back the patterned blue-green bedspread and found embroidered Egyptian cotton sheets and pillowcases.

On the side table next to the bed was a note for me on her personal note paper.

"Mr. Albert: Thank you for such a wonderful afternoon tea. It pleases me beyond words how long and how much you have loved my husband. I hope you enjoy this room as much as I do. You will find it conducive to write, but most of all, to be alone with your thoughts about your favorite country in the world. We have something in common: I love America as much as you love my Egypt. Have a wonderful time in mystical Egypt. Fond wishes, Jehan Sadat."

I sauntered around the room touching everything to see if anything stimulated my intuition. There was a separate sitting room with a chintz sofa and two matching chairs. Oil paintings and watercolors of the Impressionist period hung on the walls. End tables, Persian rugs, and an antique armoire finished the appointments. A mini-bar was stocked with sodas, champagne, fruit juices, and mineral water.

The marble bathroom had faux-gold fixtures, a large Jacuzzi bathtub, and a separate spacious shower. The bath sheets were thick and fluffy. The soaps, shampoos, and perfumes were from Paris.

I called for my luggage. I unpacked, drew a bath, and took a long and relaxing meditation in the royal tub. The mood was perfect to write in my journal. "If you don't keep track of where you've been, you'll never know where you're going," my spiritual teacher told me.

My entry was very interesting, as much for what followed as for what I wrote:

"I'm sitting here in Madame Sadat's suite feeling like royalty. I'm thinking how strange it is to feel more connected to acquaintances, travelers, and clients than I do to my family. Why would I rather travel with ten people I don't know than with my mother or brothers and sisters?"

I stopped writing, closed my eyes, and leaned my head against the sofa. I opened a porthole. Glare from the sun flooded the room with light. I got up and wiped my face with a damp cloth. I picked up the pen and began to write with no effort. The pen glided along the surface of the paper as High Self came through.

Lesson 4:

The Family Is the Karmic Mirror

My parents divorced when I was nine years old. Dad was a phi-landering father who never kept promises and a semiprofession-al baseball player whom his teammates nicknamed Ty, after Ty Cobb, the legendary "Georgia Peach" who played for the Detroit Tigers (1905 – 1926). Ty Gaulden was a drunk, a rogue, a famous womanizer who married six times, and also a kid at heart, who could flatter a turtle from its shell and make you laugh or cry, depending on his mood. When his baseball days were over, he worked in the steel mills—sweaty and dirty. After a brief period of success in baseball, he was forced to accept the harsh reality of being a laborer. Dad was an irresponsible father to us kids and a two-timing husband to his women. He died blind and consumed with cancer in 1980.

My mother Maggie was a martyr who worked as a file clerk yet raised six children in a housing project. Maggie was beautiful and bold. She could be mean and crazy. The craziness sprang from her not wanting to be a mother no matter how much she told everyone that her children were her life. That was the problem. She wanted a life without her children, but there was nothing she could do but sacrifice everything for us kids. The comedic actor and singer Bette Midler laments in one of her live performances, "I am trapped in an act not of my own choosing." That describes my mother and it is how many of us feel. Trapped, and there is nothing we can do about it. When confronted with anything she didn't want to face, Maggie would dig a hole and hide. Sober, God-fearing, she always paid her bills on time. I saw her as she was, and I would eventually see myself in her.

I have three sisters and two brothers who divided into two opposing teams when we were growing up. One side looked and acted alike and the other side could have belonged to another family. Shame-based, but honest and diligent, the siblings knew their place in the world and stayed there. I didn't. I still don't and never will. God, not social, political, or business connections, opens my doors to opportunity.

When I got sober I called my dad on the telephone to make amends. I asked him to forgive me for being a selfish, unloving son, for never calling him or remembering his birthday with a call or a card. I was amazed at how like him I was. We were both alcoholics, rambling roses, with hair-trigger tempers.

Daddy always called his sons "boy," even after Bill, Hank, and I were over forty. I'll never forget that telephone conversation on April 28, 1980:

"Boy, you were always your daddy's favorite. Where did you get that I was ashamed of you?"

"I thought it was because I didn't play sports like Bill and Hank."

Daddy had coached baseball all his life. At his death he was chairman emeritus of Little Boys' Baseball, an organization that racist white men in the South put together when Little League was forced by law to integrate.

"Anybody can play sports, boy. God didn't mean for you to be an athlete, else you wouldn't have been born with club feet. God wanted you to use your mind. Be a teacher or a writer. Hell, boy, I named you after me even though Bill was the oldest. You and I are the same: rip-roaring, hell-raising drunks."

My Dad died the day after I made amends to him. We traveled the same back roads, got into the same kinds of trouble with the law, and had the same misguided zest for living. Today I love my daddy and I miss him.

Mother's quintessential attributes of perseverance and determination rubbed off on me more after recovery than when I was growing up. Mom was a perfectionist and always asked questions to see how something could be done better. I inherited that trait as well. We have not always been the most popular, but like her, I fall asleep when my head hits the pillow. Mother was always my best friend, even when I didn't think so. Not a day goes by that I don't miss her and wish that we had had more time together.

There is no better place to see how and why you are a big phony—as inauthentic as they come—than the family scrapbook, or as we call it in our family, a trip down memory lane. Hiding in plain sight in the photo album are the goblins and ghosts—the chamber of horrors—of your childhood and beyond. On the first page is daddy, the town drunk and wife beater. Remember all the Christmases when you thought it was so funny when he fell into the tree or came home with bad company to spoil the holiday for everyone? This is not just trailer trash we are talking about here. Fancy homes resemble this nightmare as well. Craziness lives in the big house on the hill as well as on the wrong side of the tracks. Remember Mamma—she could put on a good front with company and be mean as a snake when she was the disciplinarian? Oh, there's Aunt Mary before she chased her kids out the door with a knife screaming, "I'll kill you when I catch you." That was right after she had been to Sunday school and church.

The dirty rotten shame of this journey back through the family timeline is that your parents and siblings and grandparents—aunts and uncles and cousins—are not who they have been acting like they are. The reason all of us act like we do—drinking and over-eating and addicted to sex, drugs and rock and roll is that we are sick and tired of a life we can't stand. I always say 'thank God I found booze instead of the ministry' because repressing all those anti-Jesus feelings and trying to be a good little boy drove me crazier than a loon. I needed to tear my world apart so God could help it fall into place. Being dead broke and down and out beat living a lie, until I decided to stop burying the real me with addictions and compulsions. We need a stiff shot of whiskey and another piece of pie or another run-away-from-home-vacation to get out of the false us.

The hell of the rat pack is that no one came along to free you or them from the shame that binds the whole stinking bunch to a toxic and libelous death rattle dysfunction. You can try to clean up the rap sheet of all the nasty mean fights and the unhealthy accusations one member of the mob made to the other, but it always comes back to the same cracked mirror of karma: nobody took responsibility for his actions; nobody blew the whistle on the cover-up to say "I am not playing this game anymore"; not one single twisted soul copped a plea to his shameful behavior and I'll bet my last nickel there were no amends and no one dared say, "It's my fault and I want to make amends for my behavior."

There are those of us who have a much better replay of our life growing up. Many of us have loving and supportive parents, siblings and other relatives who are kind and considerate. I know many friends and clients who make the most of the hand life dealt them, but they do run into crises that require a family pow-wow and they do screech to a halt when one of them is about to derail. There are no perfect families and there are no Snow Whites in the sisterhood. Boy Scouts are still working tirelessly toward—they have not arrived at— sainthood. The positive attributes that parents teach their children still have a karmic flavor. None of us arrives in the cradle to bless this house and everybody lives happily ever after. The family circle can be nurturing and hands-on, but there are learning curves in the best of Good Housekeeping-approved family units.

The life history I took in the first days of sobriety convinced me that I was switched at birth. I snarled, 'those people, my family, are nothing like me and I am certainly not acting out from their gene pool.' Yet when I accept the rules of karma that I must feel every single itty-bitty thing I have done to another man, woman or dog in this lifetime or a past one, I love my family and accept the part of me that is them. Personal discovery, a hard look at the inner landscape, is how I began to change. Loving the bad in my dad and the unacceptable in mom helped me forgive and love myself.

The Gaulden bloodline indicated that I would be an alcoholic like my father and his father—I am a ninth- generation drunk. But daddy and I cleaned up the Gaulden bloodline when we sobered up. My brothers and sisters don't drink. I faced the truth that I am my picky, critical, and analytical mother and I am my alcoholic, sex-addict father. My brothers and sisters taught me more humility than I would have learned in an orphanage. I cast them in the play I wrote to help me look at me.

If I don't see the changes I need to make, I will return again and again to face what I refused to look at in this life. The conditions will get rougher and tougher in each subsequent life. I am the friends and well-known people I admire, and the ones I can't stand and judge as well. When I clear away false perceptions of whom I am and live consciously daily, I clear away lifetimes of how I have misidentified myself. I Windex the family karmic mirror clean.

William Shakespeare, a master metaphysician who insinuated everything we ever need to know about the human condition in his plays, wrote in *As You like It,*

"All the world's a stage,
and all the men and women merely players.
They have their exits and their entrances,
and one man in his time plays many parts,
His acts being seven ages."

For the high brows, if you want familial toxic behavior up close, read or see a production of *Richard III, Romeo and Juliet, Macbeth, Hamlet, The Merchant of Venice,* or many of his other plays. I call them Shakespeare's mirrors, for in them we see ourselves and the messes we make in the family circle. Opera offers the same distorted and messy scenarios. Go to the Met and see a

production of *Turnadot, Tosca, Madame Butterfly, and La Bohème*
—any of these opera classics will show us what is going on in our
families.

Shakespeare suggests that the roles are somewhat beyond the
players' control and that the script for the play has already been
written by an eternal power. If all of us are actors in the plays we
write, could it be that we are in repertory theatre, first the child
and then the parent, in a subsequent life? Who am I to disagree
with Shakespeare, but I myself believe in free will. When you get
the message, start changing what you can—you. The notion that
the stage has been set and everyone has his script makes sense, if
we understand that we are here to rewrite scene after scene with
an altered consciousness and right use of will.

All of this insinuates that perhaps you *have been* your mother
and father and siblings in a previous incarnation. At the very
least, if you want to know what lessons you need to learn and
who your teachers are, look at those seated around the dinner
table. All of us are interrelated through karma and ancestrally
to our family members, and those we like least will force us to
look at our own hidden parts contained in their dark side. What
you don't like about your mother is what you find unacceptable
in yourself. If you find a lot to abhor in your father, the seed of
discontent is to be found within you.

I was working on Martha's Vineyard with Broadway producer
Manny Fox, who produced *Sophisticated Ladies,* when I crawled
into his one-year old baby William's playpen and started to sing
to him. William's grandmother said to Manny, "Albert's in show
business." Manny said, "Ma, we're all in show business."

Manny was right. We write our own scripts, and we choose
who is going to act in the play that we wrote.

There are no victims in the family chamber of horrors. Whatever your lot—unloving parents, being born into poverty—you
deserved it. What your parents do to you in this lifetime is pay-

back for what you did to them or someone else somewhere some time. You have treated them as they are treating you. From somewhere in time, you are harvesting the rotten crop you've sown. Remember you reap what you sow. Natural law demands that you feel what it felt like to inflict something on someone else. You must experience *every single thing* you've ever done to harm another. This is karmic retribution.

You need look no farther than the family tree to know what you have to clear. If daddy's a drunk, check your tolerance for alcohol. It is important to look at all addictions and compulsions. Where do you look for what's wrong with whom—and how to change? Look at nutty Uncle Eddie's antics. See momma as flawed but doing the best she can—and make a vow not to live out her defects and don't try to become her. Be you—the real you. Stare at your brother and sister until you get an eyeful of family dysfunction and toxicity. Lie, cheat, steal, and deny it all, but you'll see yourself and what you need to change by looking in the karmic mirror. Change starts with forgiving yourself and then making amends with them.

If Uncle Joe dies in a car wreck, he killed someone in another life. It may have been a chariot or a covered wagon, but Joe took a life, and had to feel what it felt like to have harmed or hurt or killed someone else. Many of us question why bad things happen to good people. Aunt Mildred never harmed a fly. So why was she raped and murdered? I believe that in a former existence, she raped and murdered someone herself.

What do you see when you look, and what do you hear when you listen? See a victim and you will become one. See a precious child of God and you'll do what you need to do to become again who God created you to be. Hear what's bad about life and how everybody's always picking on you and you'll never turn up the volume to God's divine plan for your life. The movie you're in is trying to show you the litany of what you've done that needs major altered attitude and transformation. There are no mistakes and it is show time.

DNA swears we will look like our parents at seventy, attract their diseases, lose the same amount of hair, and even embrace their habits. In the silent and invisible Upper World of supreme authority, there is a holy principle of action and reaction. If you inherited your daddy's eyes, why wouldn't you catch his laziness? If momma mistreated you, could you have been a bad mother somewhere in time?

You do not necessarily inherit all the bad or good qualities of your family. You don't become an alcoholic just because your father is. But believe you me, what you need to peel back and detox is in the house. Mother and father and everybody else you are related to has other qualities that are just as destructive, like womanizing or gambling, or you may have inherited his propensity for physical or sexual abuse. Children always share in their parents' karma. And I would be remiss not to mention that you might have been gifted with all the good qualities from mom and dad and grandparents like unselfishness, kindness, being nurturing and being temperate in all areas of their lives. We can't blame our family for the way we turn out, but we need to make a vow to change the lineage. My dad and I sobered up, the first in that ancestral tree for more than a hundred years.

In most families, one parent may be the sainted caretaker while the other uses control and fear to keep the family in tow. Momma's not always the sweet, long-suffering shoulder to lean on. Daddy sometimes is treated like a child and scolded along with the rest of the kids.

What can you do about family dysfunction? Here's my checklist:

1) Determine to get help. Everybody's sick somewhere. Oftentimes, it can be as simple as working with a life coach. In other cases, you may want to hire a licensed

psychologist or transpersonal therapist. Well people are in therapy; sick people are in denial.

2) Take a fearless and moral inventory of family secrets. It will show you where the golden aspects of the family lie as well as uncovering all the scary aspects of betrayal and distrust.

3) Resign from the debating society and stop the blame game. Look at yourself and work on you. Don't baby-sit or baby talk mom's sickness and don't carry a brother's shame.

4) Be direct. Speak truthfully and don't permit yourself or anyone else to candy-coat hurt deeds or harsh words.

5) Determine to be the family member who's come to the end of the line with family bizarre behavior and inappropriate treatment of yourself and them. Change you and clear you of this never ending chaos.

I remember a client who was a bastard child. Her mother married soon after she was born, and the new husband took the baby as his own. It was never discussed until my client, June, came to Sedona to work with me.

When she wrote about family secrets, June revealed that her mother was not married when she was born. June agonized over living more than thirty years with the big lie and secret. Telling me freed her from the prison of shame.

I had her speak to her mother when she returned home. She let her mother know that she loved her and her father, but that she wanted to be free of secrets. The communication opened locked doors of guilt, fear, shame, misunderstanding, and elicited an admission by her mother that she had secretly hated June and wished that June had never been born. And June found out that her grandmother had borne a child out of wedlock: her own mother. These two women had a glorious homecoming because one of them refused to live a lie. June faced an ego that tried to make her live a life full of fear and separation, and her ego lost.

In my brand of therapy, I have clients write themselves out of dark and dangerous places. The mind is a favorite lodge for egocentric misinformation. Stinking thinking prevents you from open and honest review.

I studied under a spiritual teacher who said that past misdeeds are caked and layered in our subconscious. He used the analogy of someone waxing a dirty floor without cleaning the dirt and grime before she applied the polish. The surface shines, but beneath is filth.

Changing the things we can starts with making direct amends to those we have harmed. Do not live your life riddled with resentments. All parties are at fault. No one is the sole culprit. Asking forgiveness for your part in a disagreement or an all-out cat fight or worse will free you. After the unpleasant business has been cleaned and cleared, practice whatever steps or daily remedies you need to stay clean and clear.

Several days later when the cruise ship docked and my group left the boat, I had a lot of treasures from my inaugural grand tour of Egypt, busts, prayer shawls, scarabs and cartouches, but none as prized as the journal I kept. Madame Sadat was the reunion that most impacted me, but what was most profound was a Solar Eclipse New Moon conjunct my sun in Pisces, which indicated that I needed to face an imposter, someone who had been using my name, using my credit cards and passport and speaking in my behalf. The imposter was Albert, but the true self, the authentic self, the real me was emerging.

Chapter 7

You're Not Who You Think You Are

Ever since my first trip to Egypt with the Flanagans, when I take tours to the land of the Nile, I stop over in Greece to cool off after the intense spiritual growth and high heat in Upper and Lower Egypt. It gives me a chance to ruminate about my journey through the world's most powerful vortex. Some say that Egypt is the epicenter of the world, and where higher consciousness originated.

I have always been amazed that Upper Egypt is in the south and Lower Egypt in the north. I chuckle to think that the Nile River can run uphill. But my life, like the Nile, is one of paradoxes In recovery, three paradoxes keep me coming back to meetings and working the steps: one is *surrender to live,* another is *die to live,* and the third is *give it away to keep it.*

The villages and tombs along the Nile are not destinations for the bored traveler. The Valley of the Kings and Queens, the Great Pyramid, the sphinx, and the temples and tombs unconsciously beckon you to die and be reborn. You intuitively recognize transcendent change.

I continued to meditate daily. Paul did not come every time I got quiet. He didn't need to. He told me that I would integrate information into my day-to-day work, for I was now hooked up to a highly intelligent energy center. I trusted. It worked.

I came to know that I am an ordinary man who had begun communicating with someone I couldn't see, touch, or feel. Most of all, I listened less to people's opinions about me or other matters that may have affected my personal worldview. My own still small voice reconfirmed that something exciting and challenging in my career was wrapped in an eclipse or hidden in my astrological birth chart. One of my mentors, astrologer Katharine de Jersey, did my chart and advised: "Keep clearing; you're not done yet!"

Astrology has taken a bad rap, particularly from the Christian right, since the dawn of institutionalized religion. Although biblical references exist to confirm how planetary movements determine character and why things happen when they do, fear keeps the preachers railing against the messages in the sky map. Respected scholars are writing books about the historical power of astrology to influence the worldview, such as the aforementioned *Cosmos and Psyche* and *The Fated Sky: Astrology in History* by Benson Bobrick.

When clients and friends asked what they could do to connect to High Self guidance, I suggested that they pray and meditate daily, and clear away the wreckage of their past and present.

Having been out of town, my mail had piled up and phone messages needed my attention. Scanning the numbers, I called Sharon Lawrence in Maui, Hawaii, who ran the speakers bureau there. She wanted me to speak at a conference on relationships the weekend after Thanksgiving. I accepted her invitation.

Maui is one of the spiritual power points in the world. Most tourists go to sun and surf and to eat the delicious Hawaiian food at luau. After you trudge the boardwalks of Lahaina, golf at Kapalua, and enjoy some deep-sea fishing and diving, the real

Hawaii awaits near the Haleakala Crater up-country and in the more remote paradises at Hana and the Seven Pools.

The tiny airport was insane the afternoon I landed on Maui. The jetliner was filled to the coat racks with pasty-white mainlanders frothing for Maui mai tai madness. When my hosts Jon and Marcia met me at the old hangar-landing field in Kahului, they were loaded down with tuberose leis.

After freshening up at the hotel, we drove to the community center in Kihei, where I was to lecture. The meeting room held two hundred people, and it would be filled that night. The Maui meeting was going to be a test for me and my new source of information.

We arrived at six o'clock. I walked along the black-sand beaches across the Kihei Highway. The sun set against a blood-red horizon. Waves gently lapped against the craggy coastline. The ocean made a soothing, rushing rhythm. This relaxing walking meditation stilled my busy mind.

As the crowds milled in, groups tended to fill in the back seats first. Quickly, I asked several high-energy people to sit in the first three rows. They would serve as strong anchors and receivers.

Technicians set up a sound system with large speakers. Flowers and trees filled the stage. The lights dimmed. I calmed down as soon as the music started. I had chosen a medley of melodic arias by Giacomo Puccini and Giuseppe Verdi, because their laments of broken dreams in operas like *La Bohème, Aïda,* and *La Traviata* were appropriate for where my lecture would take the audience.

Lesson 5:

You're Not Who You Think You Are

"Good evening, ladies and gentlemen. If you read my flyer, 'Male vs. Female—the Relationship Dilemma,' you probably know that we're gonna talk about cracked ribs, black eyes, hurt feelings, broken dreams, and one more love affair that turned deadly. Someone said to me after this same lecture in Chicago last year that I should have called it 'Welcome to Your Nightmare.'

"I am a cockeyed, bullheaded, fire-breathing optimist, and I believe that you don't quit one minute before the miracle, especially in a relationship. But I must be honest about what I know: Relationships don't work the way that you've been working them. If they're broken I suggest that you fix them or leave them.

"The reason they don't work is that two people never want the same thing at the same time. You can't have a relationship with somebody else until you have one with yourself. And you can't have one with yourself, because you don't know who you are.

"From the moment you landed on planet Earth, nobody had a clue about who you were. You were mislabeled at birth. Dress boys in blue, girls in pink? I don't think so.

"Your parents are not who you think they are either. Husbands, wives, and lovers are everything and anything but whom you think they are. All of us create the other from our own egocentric points of view. Yet it goes deeper and deadlier than that: We need for someone to inherit the unwanted, unattractive qualities within us that we refuse to face and heal.

"Unfortunately, it doesn't work that way. When we play the blame game, accusing our lover for why we feel bad, he or she should say to us, 'deal with your own anger—let me deal with my own issues.' They would say it to us if they knew how. The problem is that few of us are throwing stuff back to the other side of the fence where it belongs.

"If you're not who you think you are, and if others have been created as you need for them to be and not as they really are, who are you and who are they? We are all powerful light beings who have lost the middle ground, the psychological androgyny of consciousness, by reincarnating as a man and then a woman, changing gender randomly from one lifetime to another. But in truth we are neither male nor female—we are both.

"The first clue to where you can find the real you is in your astrological birth chart. If you're sick, go to the doctor. If you want to invest money, look for a financial advisor. If you want to know the best place to discover you, consult with a good astrologer.

"There is no big mystery here. If you want to know what is causing the bad blood in your marriage or with your live-in lover, ladies, get an astrologer to talk to you about the planets Mars and Saturn in your chart. These planets are causing you huge problems, because you won't claim the aggressive nature of Mars and the cold detachment of Saturn for yourself—you transfer them to your husband or lover. Guys find out where your Moon and Venus are, and you will uncover the irritating, unwanted bad-boy stuff you've been throwing on your gal pal's side of the aisle.

"Kabbalah teaches that who you are is in your birth chart. Kabbalistic Astrology dates back to a system of wisdom over 5000 years old, based on writings by Abraham the Patriarch. It is the oldest and most profound application of astronomy and astrology known to humankind. As practiced by the kabbalists, the study of the planets and stars is a true science through which we can understand and satisfy our deepest needs.

"When I was twenty-four, I met a woman at a party in New York named Byrd Knapp, who happened to be an astrologer. I didn't know Byrd, although we were both from Birmingham, Alabama, and I certainly didn't know what an astrologer was—

because I was a Baptist, and Baptists believed astrology was the work of the devil. My preacher told me I was supposed to be a minister. My history teacher told me I was meant to teach. My doctor said I should go to medical school, and a friend's dad who was a lawyer said I would make a good Clarence Darrow. Byrd Knapp told me exactly who I was, warts and all, and exactly what I was going to do with my life. That was forty-four years ago, and she has been right on the money, including that I was a drunk who would get sober when I was forty-one, would always spend more than I make, and would have the toughest time with relationships. Actually, Byrd told me that my best relationships would be working with clients, doing what I am doing today.

"I was in a restaurant a few years ago, and as a waiter whom I had never seen before passed my table, the still, small voice said to me, 'That's him.' Instinctively I knew that he was the young man two clairvoyants had predicted many years ago that I would meet: *When you are around sixty years old, you will meet a young man who was your son in a former life. You must help him have a better life. You owe him.*

"His name was Scott, 28 years old. He was living with a girl-friend and had recently had several sessions with a shrink, because he was drinking and drugging to excess. He was living a life he hated and didn't understand. I arm wrestled him into coming over to my house, where I did his astrology. I weighed in on who he really was, picking right up on the booze and drugs, although he tried to convince me he had been sober for a number of years. I blew his covers, took him to a meeting, and eventually hired him to work in my company. Today, Scott is my business partner. He has been clean and sober for more than nine years. All of this occurred because someone like me showed up, equipped with the true road map of who he was and what God wanted him to do with his life. Oh, and he too is training to be an astro-intuitive, because it's in his astrological birth chart.

"I have worked with thousands of people who disavowed astrology but who could not resist the truth of what their birth chart revealed—and when we pulled back the layers of the false self and all the defects of character they had to face and change, they found out who they really were. As I did in my life, we can clear away all your garbage like alcohol, drugs, food addiction, sexual addiction, greed, anger, rage, and a million forms of fear-based false selves, so you can become authentic.

"A birth chart is a treasure map of redemption. It offers you free will to make as many mistakes as you need in order to finally hit bottom so you can rise to the top. Astrology is not straight-laced or stodgy, but rather it can tell you things like what is the best career for you, when you'll meet someone special, whether or when you'll have children, and the like. Unlike religion, which dictates, or politics, which has a self-serving agenda, your birth chart can guide you through choppy waters but will always see you to safe landing when you have learned what the stormy weather was about."

The audience was restless, and the foot shakers were in full force. It was time to shift gears and take the group to the moon.

"Although the birth chart tells you where your sore spots are and ultimately who you are, you have to do a lot of work to get to the true self. Getting there is what we are doing here tonight. You must clear away a lot of misconceptions with proven tools to become who you really are.

"Before you can embrace the notion of following the light with the help of spirit guidance, you must look at the practical, feet-on-the-ground truth about what blocks you from being who God created you to be.

"Much of the answer lies in the dynamics of sexual politics. For centuries, mankind has waged a lot of wars, but none as futile as the battle of the sexes.

"Mommies and daddies don't know how to teach their little boys and girls how to make a marriage work or to have an affair to remember, because their parents didn't know anything about peaceful, loving coexistence—so they don't know. Monkey see, monkey do. It's a guessing game, and the guesses are all wrong.

"Tonight I am going to introduce you to old but new information about why a split the size of the Grand Canyon has existed for so long between men and women. The great divide is not what you're fighting over—money, property, or who gets the bigger closet. The schism that occurs in love, courtship, and marriage has to do with a failure of both partners to love, touch, feel, hold, and nurture a key relationship: the relationship with oneself. This is the partnership that can free you from the treadmill of picking the same disastrous lover over and over again.

"Carl Jung discovered that within every man is the reflection of a woman and within every woman is the reflection of a man. Jung called this reflection one's shadow. Dr. John A. Sanford, a Jungian therapist, referred to this ignored side of a person as his *invisible partner*. Dr. Sanford says in his masterpiece on the shadow, *The Invisible Partners: How the Male and Female in each of Us Affects our Relationships,* that if we refuse to recognize the invisible partner (or shadow), it can drive us to drink excessively, act out adulterously, and even commit murder.

"The female within the man is known by the Latin word *anima,* and the male within the woman is called her *animus.* You'll keep it straighter if I say the girl in the boy and the boy in the girl.

"Let's see if we can define the invisible partner in simpler language. The spirit of the invisible partner within the man acts like any ordinary woman, except that she can be heard by everyone except the man in whom she lives. The shadow wants to be able to participate in a man's life and when denied that privilege, she will act out like a spoiled child, or worse. She can cause the man to slip into a foul mood. He starts to complain and find fault with everything and everybody—it's as if he is possessed by a witch. The shadow never likes to be taken for granted, and never ignore it. This sounds as if the shadow is more trouble than it's worth—but only when transferred to someone else rather than faced. The shadow is the master therapist who can lead you into peace, balance and harmony through a balance of shadow and self, when you will let it.

"I am speaking about the feminine energy within the man, but the same applies for the woman. Liken this relationship to a puppet, the woman, having her strings tugged, and a puppeteer, the shadow, pulling the strings. The shadow will drive a woman to scream and rage at and blame her mate as a way to get the woman to realize that she is unhappy with herself; the partner may or may not be blameless.

"The shadow is saying to her: 'Look at yourself. You are getting mad at the wrong person. He's just being the man you attracted to you so you could bottom out with all your bad-girl behavior. Bond with me; let's you and me have a relationship so you can make peace with yourself. I can help you put an end to the insanity and correct these never-ending defects in relationships.'

"It's like the shadow is getting her to act out so she can observe her crazy behavior. Whenever she gets disturbed and overreacts with a partner, she is the one at fault, because she is the one raging. The fulcrum of her outburst could be pent up anger at a father or the bad blood between her and an ex-husband or an old lover. She has buried these feelings, and the shadow needles her and cajoles her to act out, as a way to get her to face the real problem. She is raging at her lover, when it is her father whom she would like to strangle.

"Her shadow is trying to help her first to survive and then to thrive by digging deep within herself until she reaches all the anger, resentment, blame, shame, and every other buried feeling that has caused her to lose at having a relationship with herself or someone else. She needs to look at the source of these feelings and heal them. Her shadow does not want her to be dependent on a man for her happiness. But she will never become independent until she gets acquainted with her invisible partner.

"I suggest to my clients that they name their invisible partners and talk out loud to them. This may seem a bit weird at first, but when it sinks in that you and your shadow are one and the same—you live the part of one gender, and the shadow represents your opposite-gender side. If you have never talked to yourself, you are missing out on one of life's greatest pleasures. The going may be a bit rougher in the beginning, but the more you engage and dialogue with your shadow, the freer you are going to be of your spouse or lover or anyone else for that matter. This is an effective exercise to let go of somebody else's garbage and, at the same time, tend to your own stinking thinking.

"You: Since my name is Mary, may I call you Marcus?

"Shadow: I prefer Marco—I am an Italian.

"You: I need some help from you, Marco. Why do my husband and I fight all the time?

"Shadow: You want something from him that only I can give you.

"You: What?

"Shadow: You are angry that you are both advertising executives but he makes more money than you do. Am I right?

"You: Yes. And he is not as smart as I am.

"Shadow: Prove your worth to your boss at work. Don't take it out on your husband at home.

"You: How can I get rid of this anger toward my husband?

"Shadow: Have a weekly powwow where you both get everything off your chests and out in the open, where you can discuss troubling issues and resolve hidden resentments. If you do this, your resentments will disappear and you will remember the real reasons you married your husband in the first place.

"I could go on forever, but I think you get the idea. You are resolving many of the key issues in your marriage or with your partner by getting honest with yourself. These kinds of chats with your shadow are how many of us learn to distinguish between what we can change and what we are powerless to change. We can only change us.

"The invisible partner can either be ignored or integrated. In order to become whole you must embrace your ego, which is the way to holism, for ego and the shadow are synonymous—they are the same troublemakers. When you make the shadow a friend, it becomes an ally in balancing your internal world.

"Because we are unaware of this unseen personality, we don't know to get acquainted with our shadow. Instead we unconsciously project the shadow onto the one we love, and then the transference breeds contempt. We deny that a quality like jealousy or passive-aggressive behavior is ours, so we convince ourselves that these unattractive character defects describe the other person. I suggest you talk and talk and talk to your shadow until you get good positive results from the collaboration.

"I had a Gentle Ben client named Mike who was married to Misty, a woman who was all Victoria's Secret and *Desperate Housewives,* until her masculine side acted up. Then Misty became more of a man than Mike.

"Misty had low self-esteem, hated her father, and thought her mom was a doormat. She jogged five miles a day, took aerobics and yoga classes, excelled in martial arts, read self-help books, and nagged Mike to attend every lecture on relationships. But nothing ever got better with Mike and Misty. They blamed each other for what didn't work and never saw their parts in what was wrong with their marriage.

"Mike had a dictator for a daddy. Nothing Mike ever did was good enough. Mike's mom was schizophrenic and died when he was young. Finding the right woman became an obsession for him, for he needed someone soft, soothing, and tender to tell him he was okay.

"Where did the marriage break down? Mike never found a woman to replace his mother. A wife is not a mother and can never heal what a mother couldn't or didn't. His passive-aggressive behavior was masking fear of confronting what was wrong with him.

"If Misty didn't like her father, she wasn't going to find a husband to make her happy. She was unconsciously running old tapes that affected how she felt about men generally. And plastic surgery never healed soul sickness. But a good, honest inventory of our character flaws, including past wrongs to others, can do wonders to heal what hurts and to save ourselves and our relationship.

"How could the relationship between Mike and Misty have healed and gotten better? He could have acknowledged that he had always looked for a woman to fix him and been honest with Misty that he didn't know how to have a relationship. She could have owned up to looking for a man to resolve the hatred she felt for her father. He could have confessed how he used people, places, and things to deaden the pain of how unloved he felt. And she could have begun the healing process by looking at how much she was trying to fix her inner self by working frantically on the outside.

"Once we wake up to what we are doing and recognize that our irritations are about us and not someone else, we can no longer project our unattractive, unwanted negative qualities onto our significant relationships. Projections are always unconscious. When you become conscious, you must face what's wrong with you.

"One of the major reasons we are not able to make a partnership work is that these projected qualities keep getting in the way of peaceful coexistence. Since God created Eve from Adam's rib, the shadow has kept causing trouble because it wants to be recognized, to be a part of our lives, to become integrated into our outward personality, but it never has been. It wants to save us, but we won't let it.

"Who among us has ever been told to value his dark side? Who among us has ever acknowledged the sheer power of the sinister underbelly of his soul? Who of us has ever realized that he can't have a relationship with someone else because he has never had one with all of himself? Let the shadow tell you about your own shortcomings, so that you can amend them. Permit the shadow to take you to scary places where you will not like what you see. In a moment of clarity, who you really are—the proverbial "aha"—will flash before your eyes as a result of looking more honestly at yourself. My dark side teaches me more than all the hot lights of Heaven. The shadow will drive you to look at your bondage, but it is the High Self who liberates you.

"'Is she gay or isn't she?' 'Is he gay or isn't he?'" These questions have a life of their own. Curiosity about someone else's sexuality really points to questions you have about your own sexual identity. Within the middle ground where androgyny lives, we can find answers to confusion about 'Am I or am I not?'

"Major cities and small towns as well are full of married men and women who have a same-sex lover on the side. Oprah Winfrey did a television show called 'Living on the Down Low,' about this very topic: men who have sex with other men but keep their wives and girlfriends as cover-ups. I wish I had a dime for all the straight men I have worked with who have had sex with another man—one-night, two-night, a-lot-of-night stands. These men run into one another in dark parks and seedy bars, and at exclusive country clubs. Would you believe there are a lot of sex hook-ups on football fields and in gymnasiums and other male-only domains?"

Gary J. Gates, a demographer at the Williams Institute, a research group that studies gay issues at UCLA, found that as high as 38 percent of gay men have been married. Of 27 million married men, Mr. Gates found that 1.6 percent, or 436,000, said they were gay or bisexual. He cites Cole Porter and former governor of New Jersey James McGreevey as men who are married and yet have relationships with a man or men on the side.

An article in the *New York Times* dated August 4, 2006, called "When the Beard Is Too Painful to Remove," lists two websites that deal with the phenomenon of married men having sex with other men: **www.marriedgay.org** and **www.gayhusbands.com**, the second maintained by Bonnie Kaye, the former wife of a gay man. Kaye conducts "How to Come Out to Your Wife" workshops.

"Much of this behavior stems from the homophobic society we are raised in. As long as fathers keep trying to make their sons stud athletes and moms insist their daughters act and dress like beauty queens, the imbalance is going to create more closeted kids who grow up to express their sexual desires no matter what they might be.

"Gender studies are proliferating in colleges and universities around the country, instigated by young people dying to know who they are and how to express themselves in sexual relationships or fantasies. They seem to be saying to all of us, 'Wait a minute: something about what I have been taught about my sexual identity doesn't compute. Something is rotten in Denmark.'

"The issue here is that most of us are terrified to look at who we are sexually. To our way of thinking, people are either gay or straight. How about posing this question: 'What would my life look like if I were both heterosexual and homosexual? How would my happiness quotient skyrocket if sexual preference was not the be-all and end-all of who I am? And what if it was more natural to live as a man or a woman with the androgyny of consciousness as opposed to either one or the other?'

"Men and women these days are entering into "spiritual love" relationships without the sexual component. They seek a deep bond without the confusion and diminishing effects of sexual politics. We call this phenomenon agape love, or Zen love. Women especially have found greater comfort, tenderness, caring, and safety with other women than they have experienced in staying put with their boyfriends or husbands.

"As a case in point, Oprah recently said that she and close friend Gayle King are not gay; they are not lovers. In her statement, Oprah said, 'There isn't a definition in our culture for this kind of bond between women. So I get why people have to label it—how can you be this close without being sexual?' Winfrey went on to add, 'Something about this relationship feels otherworldly to me, like it was designed by a power and a hand greater than my own. Whatever this friendship is, it has been a very fun ride.'

"I agree with Oprah about her relationship with Gayle. There are a lot of deep friendships between women and women and men and men that seem like soul mates and not bed partners. Oprah has settled into a comfort zone of love without sex that so many people have begun to embrace.

"If I knew Oprah, I would tell her to say to anyone who asked if she were gay: 'Do you need for me to be?' That would throw the light of inquiry back on the person who really would like to ask herself that question, but can't or won't.

"I have a forty-something-year practice dealing with people who have been confused about themselves and those they consider date bait. It is not what someone brings to a relationship, gay or straight, that makes you whole and happy. It is what you allow yourself to give to yourself.

"I had a California client a few years ago who eventually divorced her husband because he wouldn't let their son Josh take ballet lessons. The father, a football coach, said, 'No son of mine is going to put on a pair of tights and flit around on a stage for his family and friends to see. Little boys play sports; girls dance.'

"The son was allowing his softer side to express itself, but because his father had always undervalued and denied his own feminine side, the father projected his homophobia onto his son.

"Josh became a leading dancer in one of the country's finest ballet companies. I had lunch with Josh after he became a *premier danseur,* and he told me that his father—the all-man football coach who had shamed his son about ballet—had sexually molested him and his older brother from the age of five until they left for boarding school when they were eighteen.

"'Your father transferred his shadow to you, refused to deal with his dark side, and his shadow drove him to act out sexually with you,' I told Josh.

"A recurring theme in my counseling with men and women is sexual abuse by an adult when the client was four or five or six years old. The abuse often continues into adolescence and longer. Many women have been sexually violated by their fathers and brothers. I could write a book about the women I know whose fathers sexually abused them for ten to fifteen years without anyone ever knowing. It only stopped when the young women went off to college. Boys have had the same inappropriate touching by adult men. Catholic priests are not the only men who have scarred young boys and girls. John Bradshaw, considered by many in the field of transpersonal psychology to be the father of the personal-growth movement, wrote about childhood sexual abuse and how its denial set us up for a life of never-ending torment in *Family Secrets: What You Don't Tell Can Hurt You.*

"So the first danger that transference creates out of fear is that the forgotten side of us will rattle its cage and come out in the most inappropriate ways. We need to see that what we don't like in our partner can benefit us if we claim the unattractive traits as our own, and deal with them. A weekly powwow with our partner can open the door to healing our breakdowns and their root causes. Play the blame game with your partner, and you will lose every hand. Change you and change the kind of relationships you attract.

"When unintegrated, an invisible partner can create havoc and mayhem. When a man denies that a shadow of a woman lives within him, the shadow self will cause trouble. If a woman never turns to consult the man within her, who is the only man in her life who can free her of polarity projections, her invisible partner will drive all available relationships away.

"Talk to a recovering drunk and see how many times he ended up in bed with a stranger. Ask him about his credit rating or career history. How many marriages? Our shadow drives us into these insane debaucheries. We cannot afford to marginalize the kind of power our invisible partner wields. It renders us pitifully and incomprehensibly demoralized.

"Remember that poem by Robert Louis Stevenson that you learned as a kid: 'I have a little shadow that goes in and out with me....'? No matter how much we try to get someone else to live out our character defects by projecting them, they stick to us like chewing gum to a shoe. Or they boomerang back where they belong.

"The concept of an invisible partner is new to most of us. If you don't face the fear of what this invisible partner business is all about, you'll live with bad marriages, sink under huge alimony payments, or end up raising kids alone as a single mom. These things will happen because you keep doing the same thing, expecting different results.

"Dumb Dora from Alabama that I am, I concluded that the reason men and women fight, kick, curse, and get divorced all the time is that the girls are the boys and the boys are the girls."

The audience roared with laughter and recognition. "And if you're gay, don't let yourself off the hook with nervous titter. Gay relationships have the same issues as do straight couples. Homosexual people, in their struggle to be who they are and love who they choose, seem to ape straight behavior in relationships. Homosexual men and women adopt children, get married where it is legal, and stay together or break up just like heterosexual couples. But gay men and women are given more grief about their sexuality, because straight people are terrified to deal with what they perceive to be such a dark part of them. Heterosexual men transfer their homosexuality onto homosexual men. Women are a bit more sympathetic and empathetic to gay men and women. But when the church weighs in on homosexuality, gay men and women are condemned.

"Anytime you mention gay anything, everybody gets real uncomfortable.

"Medical science says that we are all born bisexual. Either genetics or experience determines which side of the 'bi-' you become.

"The hot-button issue of invisible partners is not about sexual preference. Whether we're gay or straight or gay and straight makes no difference—both are illusions that hide true feelings. Until we integrate or balance our shadow—or invisible partner—with ourselves, who we live with and love doesn't matter. We are going to have the same defective no-win partnership, whether homosexual or heterosexual.

"You are neither gay nor straight. You are both. You choose the sex partner who best satisfies you karmically. Don't judge someone for the choice they make.

"Women seem to prefer a partner who is softer, gentler, kinder, sweeter, and more loving. The jock who bowled her over in high school or college proved that his right stuff was on the ball field and not necessarily in a loving and balanced marriage. Besides that, we are seeing more and more professional athletes being charged with spousal abuse—all because they don't know how to pick a fight with the one they're really mad at—themselves.

"Men are acknowledging that their wives are as talented and as tough in business as men are and should be paid equally. Professional tennis is still squabbling over equal pay for the ladies. Male and female tennis players are paid the same at the U.S. Open, but men are paid more at Wimbledon. The good old boys' network was a manifestation of repression of a man's anima, which led to fear that women would show men up in the boardroom.

"We can integrate the parts of ourselves that engage in destructive behavior, such as spousal abuse, sexual abuse, gay bashing, and violence toward people of color, so that we can live and let live. The first step to integration, resolving the problem with the shadow, is to accept that part of us, to make friends with the shadow in order to heal.

"For clarification, in my experience, homophobia is fear that you are gay, not repulsion of someone who is. If you don't deal with your repressed homosexuality, your relationships will be total projection and no satisfaction.

"Since we are really all-knowing androgynes, we cannot become who we really are until we balance our outward identity with our inner shadow selves. We are not capable of bonding with the man or woman of our dreams, because the nightmare of separation from self won't let us.

"Are some of us able to balance our diverse natures and live happily as heterosexual men or women? And is true love possible for a homosexual woman or man? The answer to both questions is a resounding, 'Yes!'

"Let's turn to Carl Jung for insights into how to find the authentic self—the one who can make us truly happy. He says that the only way to become the true self is to be individuated—to move away from herd mentality and the opinions of others to make up our own minds about who we are and what we believe for ourselves.

"Did you ever stop to think why a brilliant poet like Emily Dickinson would live in self-imposed exile from her fellowman? Have you a clue why spiritual teachers live in monasteries and geniuses like Nietzsche hide where we can't find them? They have been so individuated that they do not want to hear from those of us who are still immersed in the annoying fray, drawing attention to ourselves like the women of the 19th century who were so desperate to be noticed that they walked about with a monkey on a stick. They needed attention because they could not recognize their own intrinsic value.

"Okay, so now you have taken a hard look at the real culprit in your failed relationships—yourself. But what's next? What can you do to change you to be able to have a good solid partnership with another person?

"Get honest with yourself, and stop rationalizing bad-boy, bad-girl behavior. Surrender to the notion that you'll never change anyone but yourself, then start to deal with your own issues and let the other person deal with his or hers.

"Since I was tall enough to get Miss Cooper's attention in the first grade, I have been asking tough questions. So I ask you, 'If your relationship isn't working, why do you stay in it?' Could your answer be 'because everybody else is in a relationship'? Or 'because it's expected of me'? Or how about, 'because I don't want to be alone'? These responses are not good enough and will only keep you sick and tired of the matches you make.

"The paradoxes and the impossibilities of partnership are to be found in the golden aspects of the shadow. We all must unlearn a lot of behavior that has kept us mired in the defeat of failed partnering.

"So how do you accept the shadow? How do you balance this dynamic that is an invisible but powerful part of you? And when you do, how will your life change?

"One: Have a conversation with your shadow daily. And don't forget to name him or her. Ask questions and listen quietly for the answers.

Two: Look at your sexuality with an open mind. Get in touch with your femininity if you are a man and your masculine side if you are a woman. Be courageous enough to face any latent homosexuality or bisexuality. A life history of all your sex partners will go a long way in sorting out patterns in why relationships have not worked for you. The American tragedy is that few of us have succeeded in finding inner peace and contentment, no matter what our sexual preference. Do some deep introspection about you and how you can be happy, joyous, and free being in a relationship with yourself.

"Three: Stop looking for Momma or Daddy in a relationship. Most people are unconsciously trying to find someone to take care of them or someone to care take of. They want the man/woman in their life to do what only their invisible partner can do.

"Four: Men, stop saying, 'I can't do that—it's not manly.' Women, accept that you can do most anything a man can do.

"Five: Communicate with your partner instead of talking at him or her. Communication should reflect a sensibility and consciousness that is androgynous, and not male-or female-slanted.

"Six: Stop people pleasing or caring what others think about how you live, think, or speak.

"Seven: Do the deep-tissue-issue work by writing a life history, an inventory of all the troubling people and events that have misshapen your perception of you and your relationships. See in black and white where the stinking thinking started and let a trusted counselor help you remove these dark spots.

"Eight: When you take these steps, the kind of man or woman you draw into your life will change. You will magnetically attract more balanced relationships. You get what you deserve. It's the law of attraction.

"Mate with the only one who can get you back to God. Love yourself.

"All you've got to do to free yourself from the trap of ego-based desires is to stop playing the game. Refuse to get into compulsive, obsessive death-spiral relationships. The next time a guy asks you to hop in the sack for a night of fun, tell him that your insurance for careless sex quit paying off. Say no ... hell no.

"The more you choose to clean and clear relationship stinkos out of your life, the closer you'll get to self-esteem and self-worth. And don't forget, the sooner you'll get home.

"Any questions? Anybody want to leave? Are we having fun yet?"

I had succeeded in getting in the faces of the sun-baked, surfing, huffing and puffing boys and girls of Maui with stark reality and irrefutable truth. They raised their hands to ask questions and jumped to their feet to deride themselves for years of failed love. It could have turned into a free-for-all, but I went with whatever the group needed to express. I knew that many of these islanders were exorcising their demons in this public place. Not one man or woman seemed to feel embarrassed by their public outbursts, and no one seated around them rebuked them for their loud displays. After a few minutes of the purging, I signaled for everyone to sit back down.

"Man, I love the honesty in this room tonight. I honor those of you who found the courage to jump in with your angst and agony. Don't stop waking up and speaking out. After the meeting tonight, sit with a friend and continue the discussion.

"Accept the fact that nobody's gonna make you happy but you. Look at the poor examples for love that you got from your parents. No matter how you disdain your mother for being a doormat or your dad for being a bully, you have the same issues, whether you know it or not. Your parents imprinted you, and you can't escape their rotten qualities until you rewire your thinker and redraw your blueprint. Talk about what lengths you went to for love. Mention gay love, straight sex, group sex—and don't forget Dr. Strangelove.

"Men have more trouble accepting their femininity than do women the male within. Tell a woman that she's predominantly masculine in actions and mind-set, and she accepts it and is often flattered. A man immediately defends his masculinity and declares his heterosexuality. This is his insecurity and discomfort with his softer side.

"A client of mine from Texas says that he is so comfortable with masculine-feminine energies that before he was born he couldn't decide whether to be male or female. At the last minute he chose to be a boy, so the angels had to stick on a little pee-pee before he came down the birth canal.

"I used to say that a bad woman is better than a good man. I stopped saying that when I started looking at the dynamics of my own invisible partner and inventorying my own sexuality. When I admitted to all the anonymous and nefarious encounters I had had, I came into a clear spot where the androgyny of consciousness lived.

"Are you getting the horror picture of what we've all been through? Can you believe that we could steer our own canoe of life across the River Styx with such fear, denial, desire, and confusion, and with no role models?

"Face all of your addictions and get help. If it's food, read *It's Not What you're Eating, It's What's Eating You*, by Janet Greeson, and then choose a therapist, a gym, and a new way to eat. For booze and drugs, join Alcoholics Anonymous or Narcotics Anonymous. All addictions have support groups.

"You'll keep attracting a partner who will mirror all the addictions and defects you are in denial about. Clean and clear before you look for a lover.

"Make it okay to be alone. Go to parties and even be willing to travel unescorted. If you define your life only through relationships, you'll draw the wrong one every time the partner cards are dealt.

"Reconnect to a relationship with a power greater than yourself. God will put the perfect partner in your life when He is ready for you to have one. Or … you may find that a relationship with yourself is all you need. The greatest fallacy is that everyone should be in a relationship or married. Some of us were born to be alone. And before I forget it, not everyone is supposed to or wants to be married. When I look out at the landscape of life and see all the misery in marriage, I wonder why so many do it.

We took a break. The audience mobbed me with questions and wanted private intuitive astroanalytical appointments. I had the booking agent set up times for each person who wanted to see me. All wanted to check out how I felt about their husband or wife or lover.

As factions of the audience broke into small gabfests, I found a small, soundproof room in which to evaluate the evening and to meditate. An ornate Egyptian daybed with chipped gold leaf and imitation stones of turquoise, coral, carnelian, and lapis lazuli sat in the corner, piled with thrift-store junk. Cool, Egypt in Hawaii.

As I lay my head down, I stared into the face of a moon-shaped clock. I relaxed but free-floated with impressions from the lecture and held a review with myself.

Boy, have I succeeded in pushing a lot of buttons, but I am concerned that they may not be getting it. What more can I share that will let them know that all of us have been trying to retrieve that lost part of ourselves for many lifetimes? "They'll hear when they hear and see when they see," a still, small voice whispered to me.

Whether the audience understands tonight that men and women are basically the same is none of my business. I plant a seed, and eventually some of them will get help.

I believe that the root cause of all emotional pain is the divided and unindividuated self. As medical records are carried in the bloodline, so too are all past actions for which we must atone. Alcoholics, drug addicts, and compulsive souls of all sorts oftentimes must die for their disease. Each of us knew the requirements of atoning for past behaviors when we chose to be reborn.

The ego starts as an imp but grows into a demon determined to keep us from God's will and God's divine plan. The only way to become who and what you were born to be is to face the ego and ask it: "Are you a devil who chases me or an angel who has come to help me?" And in that moment of truth, in compliance with natural law, the ego must die and be reborn as the precious child of God within you. Make friends with your ego. The ego is not your enemy.

We can learn from the past, but we would do well to live in the present. Now is where our problems are, and now is the time to do something about them.

The end of the line for the ego will come when you have suffered enough. Pain is the touchstone of growth. Agony causes you to go inside and take a look at who can save you: your shadow. Joy and happiness are the results of taking a close look at what you did to harm others and making direct amends to those people. It is God's pleasure for everyone to be happy, joyous, and free. Man has a choice to make: slavery to the ego, or freedom.

If only I could always remember that I am not the message, but the messenger, I thought. Tonight is not about spiritual spin, razzle-dazzle, or wrapping clearing-and-changing in a neat package. Each man and each woman will shift in his or her own time. Tonight is a new beginning about how to look at ourselves with honesty, open-mindedness, and willingness to change in order to heal our relationships.

At 9:30 sharp, I walked back into the room. Groups reassembled chairs and sat down. They seemed spellbound for God-knew-what to come.

"This has been an incredible evening for me as I hope it has been for you. I have been in your energy field all night and I resonate with the efforts you each are making to change yourselves. You have helped me to stay out of God's way by the thought impressions you have been sending me. At the break, the committee in my head was talking all at once: 'Will they get it or won't they?' 'What more can I do to make them understand better?' The quiet little voice, when all the jabbering committee shut up, said softly: 'It's none of your business, Albert.'

"It takes great courage to come to terms with the enemy within. Wherever each of us goes, we will never see spouses, mates, or lovers the same again.

"Before we leave tonight I want to introduce you to the magical, mystical world of coincidences, synchronicities, gut reactions, hunches, omens, intuitions, and all the miraculous manifestations God uses to steer us through life. When you live as someone you are not, using addictions and compulsions to cover up your true identity, you cannot enter the sizzling wonderment of God's messaging system. God's way of reaching us requires that we take all the static out of our lives—whether it be blame, anger, resentment, greed, selfishness, bullying, manipulating, or controlling. The real you is buried beneath the rubble of all the things you did to maintain being who you were not. Clean up the dump pile and rescue the precious child of God who wears the ID bracelet, whose DNA matches who you were born to be.

"I am asked constantly why my life is so magical, an observation that often engenders jealousy from others. I say that it is a matter of switching phone service. Listen to your own voice of intuition. Discover you, and you will hook up to an energy force field that draws to you the right job when you need it, a good solid relationship when you are ready, and a debt counselor when you want more black ink in your life than red.

"I have a client named Larry who is in his '70s. He recently moved to North Carolina. Larry has survived heart problems and cancer. He is a poster boy for living in the world of God's magical kingdom: when Larry needed to buy a house, someone called that very day and took him to the perfect neighborhood. If Larry needs to fill his coffers, a big order comes his way. If he needs to change directions, like not move into a certain neighborhood, the developer gives him back his deposit. Larry asks a question, and God sends a flash card. He has gone from being negative and resentful to being joyful. How has he done it? Larry has become amenable to living life with a different set of principles. Yes, he accepted guidance from me and others, but he was ready to trade in a life of misery for one loaded with laughter, love and a lot of fun. Pain got him there.

"Not everyone is willing to pay the price for the magic, because a lot of us choose to wallow in self-pity and nibble at crumbs while a banquet lies before us. It is a matter of caring too much what others think, not doing the work to change, and being unwilling to use the tools to uncover, discover, and discard—or to retain some of the good stuff.

"I would like to acknowledge and honor you for having the courage to change the things you can. When I still the mind and go into a relaxed and meditative state, I play 'let's pretend,' like I did when I was a kid. I talk and argue sometimes with an inner presence that I call Paul. When my mind is cluttered and my ego has me in its vise, Paul has to do most of the talking.

"Tonight when you were in groups decoding and deciphering relationships, I was in the back room getting a message for you.

"The winding road back home is long and forlorn. Your reason for coming back to Earth is to right wrongs, to feel what it feels like to make better choices, and to reclaim your birthright. You pick a friend so the journey will be less lonely and because the partner mirrors the adjustments that you need to make.

"A child is born. A soul makes a contract with a man and woman to return as their child in need of redemption. Parenting is a school program for souls to face karma.

"Each of us is on a path to return home. God waits for us to make a choice to clear away all blocks, barriers, and impediments to remembering who we really are. Relationship difficulties are the major pitfall to clearing.

"Within you is a consciousness that can speak to you, that can guide you toward the kingdom of Heaven. Get quiet. Be still. Listen for the note and see the colors that will lead you to your clearing. Hear the voice that will escort you home."

As I finished, a hush fell over the meeting hall. In a split second, lightning flashed through the skies outdoors. Lights dimmed, brightened, dimmed, and then the brightness intensified inside the building. The audience gasped; many sobbed. A plain-faced middle-aged woman began to sing a hymn.

"This little light of mine, I'm gonna let it shine;
This little light of mine, I'm gonna let it shine..."

Men and women began to sing softly and then with great gusto. They stood and began to file out, one by one, and then in groups.

Chapter 8

Forgiveness

Five days later at six o'clock in the morning, I left Maui. On the plane to Los Angeles, I read, I catnapped, and I listened to tapes. Intuitively I knew my life was about to shift into high gear. Detachment guided me. The still, small voice whispered, "Live and let live." Purpose, not outcome, became my watchword. How something turned out was God's business, not mine.

I have always been a people person. I get high from travel, reconnecting with people I've known before and remembering ideas that seem like ancient memories. "Tell me something I don't know" is my mantra. To think that I am not who I think I am and that the family mirrors what I need to change in me blows me away.

"Excuse me," said a beautiful blond lady with big brown eyes seated next to me.

"Yes, what can I do for you?" I asked, turning to give my seat mate my full attention.

"I'm Lorraine May. I heard you speak in Kihei. Is sitting next to you today a meaningful coincidence or what? I'm a big Carl Jung fan, so nothing surprises me anymore.

"I loved when you said that men and women are the same. But I had a lot of questions when you were through. I know a married couple who has worked with you," she continued, "and they say that you helped save their marriage. You said in your lecture that relationships don't work. I got the impression that we should never get married at all. Got any more information for someone who would really like to have a loving and supportive relationship?" Lorraine pleaded her point of view.

"First of all, Lorraine, I did not say relationships don't work. What I said was if they're not working you had better fix them. Getting to know your shadow self is a prerequisite to having a partnership with someone else. I do honor relationships that are between two people who are balanced within themselves, people who want a partnership but don't need one. Needy, needy, needy makes my skin crawl. Relationships take a lot of work, and most of us are lazy. If you have the stamina to stay the course, you may find someone who clicks for you. For me, I want to know why 63% of marriages in this country end in divorce. If my kid came home from school with a grade of 37%, I would know he had failed the course. It is the same with relationships.

"Be honest, Lorraine. So few relationships are worth having," I said.

"So you're not saying that relationships can never work?" Lorraine hammered home hard.

"The reason you can't hear what I am saying is that your ego has you in fear gridlock. Ego screams, 'Run, Lorraine. This man wants to sentence you to a life of loneliness.' Rather I want you to quit doing the same thing and expecting different results. The true partner lives in you. Relationships work if you work at them. Unlike what we learn from society, finding men and women who can bond without enmeshment, co-dependency, or transference of negative qualities onto the other is a huge challenge. Most of us are in karmic, high-price-to-pay bondage partnerships. I assure you that the reason most of us are in relationships is because we have been conditioned to seek them no matter how rotten they are.

"Lorraine, finding someone you adore who loves you without a lot of baggage is what life is all about. However, getting married is not for everyone, and falling in love is falling for make-believe.

"Clean up your karma, do your homework on what you need to change about you, and then wait patiently to see who God brings into your life. Perhaps someone was born to be with you. But first, you must clear away the wreckage of past failed partners."

"I get it, Albert," Lorraine said. "I realize that I need to have a relationship with me without a man deciding for me who I am and what I should do with my life. Our culture seems to define us through our marriages and children. First, I need to be who I want to be. I need to do what makes me happy. A man can wait. I want someone to share my life who fits who I am inside."

"Lorraine, Ram Dass used to say, 'When you get the message, hang up the phone.'"

We embraced a last time and walked off the plane together, heading in different directions. I found Starbucks and ordered a café latte.

I closed my eyes and waited for silent guidance. What to do next? A different reality was crystallizing, and I felt compelled to go to any length to get to the essence of it.

I picked up the phone and called the Vedanta Society.

"Hello, this is Ramapriya. Who am I speaking to, please? ... Amrita? ... I need to see Swami this afternoon, if at all possible ... Yes, I'll hang on."

She left me on hold for several minutes. I really needed to see Swami Swahananda. We all need someone to run our ideas by before we act on them.

"Yes, I'm here ... He will ... Thank God. Yes, I will stay for dinner, if you'd be so kind," I said gleefully.

I called home to retrieve my voice mail. One message caught my attention: "My name is Corinne Bennett. I need to talk to you about a paranormal experience I had. I live in Beverly Hills. Please call me as soon as possible."

She left a number, so I telephoned immediately. Since I was a few miles from where she lived, we agreed to meet at Hamburger Hamlet on Sunset Boulevard.

Corinne was waiting as I walked in the door. We asked for a table in the back room. She got to the point of the meeting within minutes.

"Albert, I want to talk to you about my near-death experience. Two people I know said they had consulted with you on similar matters. I got your number from one of them. Since they didn't know each other, I took that as a meaningful coincidence and called you in Sedona. You just happened to be coming through LAX. You just happened to call home for your messages. Here we are. It all fits what I need to share with you," Corinne said nervously.

"I am happy to be of assistance, if I can. My mother had a near-death experience twenty years ago, and many of my clients have gone over and come back, but I have not," I shared.

"I had a car wreck six months ago. An elderly woman hit me on the driver's side of my car—I never saw her coming. I went through a tunnel and was met in the light on the other side by someone I knew who had died, named Elton. I was so happy to see him and to be there that I did not want to come back to Earth. Elton said that I had to return, because it was not my time to die.

"Since the accident, I see people here on Earth as light or dark. Elton and I communicate mind to mind, and he says that when I see bodies as dark beings, those souls do not know who they are; when I see light beings, those know their true identity and are headed in the right direction.

"A being that had no form—merely a mass of brilliant white light—told me that I would meet a man who needed confirmation of a life-altering shift in consciousness leading up to 2012. When my friends told me about you, I knew this heavenly creature was talking about you."

She smiled slightly, "I know it's you because I see you as light, not as body."

Corinne did not know about the lessons and my work with Paul. Human that I am, I was both shocked and grateful to hear what she had to say.

"Your experience is very fascinating and believable. But how can I help you?" I asked.

"First, can you relate to my message for you?" she asked.

"Yes, it resonates with me. I am gathering data and information that redefines how we see ourselves here on Earth, and there are indications that time is of the essence. I have accepted the challenge to let people know that they need to get home. Home is a pure and clear place within, where God lives."

We each ordered a Cobb salad and iced tea, and continued talking.

"Every word you say makes sense, but none of it would have, had I not had the near-death experience. When I came back, I was different in every way. I am a double Capricorn, so you know I am slow and deliberate and the last person on Earth to be trendy."

"Don't worry about the Capricorn business, Corinne. I look Aries but think like a Taurus. Continue, please," I said, eyeing a big slab of chocolate cake with melting marshmallow and vanilla fudge ice cream dripping off the plate.

"Albert, now that I am a changed person, what do I do with myself? My friends are used to the old me. Some days I wish I could die and go back where I was so happy," Corinne said, sobbing into her large linen luncheon napkin. I took her hand and held it and said nothing for a few moments.

"Corinne, this new consciousness will bring you even greater joy. You said that you were told to bring messages back to people. The message you have given me is of great benefit. Being aware of what others don't know is a lonely path until you meet someone who understands what you know to be true for you," I said, not so much to console her as to identify who she truly was.

"Do what you've always done. Work where you work. Stay married to your husband. Redecorate your home, if the soul urge is to change the colors in your life.

"Sound and light are our connections to God and unity. When you hear someone speak, you will intuitively know whether or not he is an ally. The resonance of his voice will also tell you if he is ready to know what you have to say.

"Prisms of colored light and meditation enhance healing. I feel your home is about to have a makeover," I said.

"You're right. She's going from being Oriental geisha to an antique Italian signora," Corinne advised.

Of course we ordered piles of chocolate pecan swirl cake topped with ice cream and hot fudge. We ate our sinful treat in silence, nodding pleasurably with each bite. Then Corinne engaged my intuition with a question: "Do you have anything else to share with me?"

"Don't live in the past. Bring what you found there, here, and share when it's safe. See it with the excitement of a child waiting for Christmas. Apocalypse and Armageddon have been waged from the first bite of that proverbial apple, and will continue until all bodies become light.

"Be the angel that you are. Be the light."

We stood up and hugged. "This is exactly what I needed to hear. Thank you, Albert," Corinne said.

"No, Corinne, thank you for bringing Heaven to Earth. Ain't it great to know that you're not who you think you are?" I asked.

When I arrived at the Vedanta Center, Swami and the nuns and monks were in a meeting.

The compound, located a stone's throw from the Hollywood Freeway, is buffered from the chaos of tinsel town by high hedge-rows. You cross the threshold to Vedanta from a large parking lot through a small opening in the shrubs. Sidewalks meander through formal gardens and lawns that surround a bookstore, the temple, a dining room, and housing for the staff and Swami. Swami's quarters are modest. A permanent fragrance of rose or lavender permeates the room where he counsels devotees. But it is the kinetic energy of Swami himself, bathed in his calm presence, that immediately alters my emotional and mental bodies. I sit with an Indian man whose accent I barely understand, yet I identify with what he has to say to me.

"From the sound of your urgent request, you must be on a slippery slope, Ramapriya. You're not crying wolf, are you?" asked Amrita.

"No, but I am in a 'narrow is the way and straight is the gate' state of mind. Thanks for setting up this time with Swami," I said.

"Don't mention it," she said. "Next time, don't forget to bring one of those five-layer triple-chocolate cakes from Hamburger Hamlet. Okay, Ramapriya?"

And with that Amrita opened the door and I stood facing my guru. We embraced. Once I asked Swami why the other devotees took his dust but I hugged him instead. "It may be a path to humility for them. Your way is to embrace me."

Swami Swahananda motioned for me to sit. I waved away the black tea and sat with a heavy sigh.

"I am not who I think I am," I blurted out.

"Then tell me who you are not," he said with that sly smile of his.

"You know that I communicate with Paul," I stated.

"Yes, and I approve of him, because he is an aspect of yourself which you call Paul to distinguish between what your clear self is saying and how your deceitful ego is trying to dupe you. But you, Ramapriya, I don't know if you hear what Paul is saying," Swami responded with a bit of irony.

"I have been given another spiritual lesson. I wanted to run it by you, to see if I am hearing correctly."

"Start at the beginning, Ramapriya. Tell me the first lesson. Explain it in your words, and then the next one, and so on," Swami said.

"Lesson one is the ego is not the enemy. The ego was born when man refused the light from God. God and the ego and I are as one. The ego is that part of me that separated from God and is an original fallen angel."

"The ego is also a positive and powerful force to get us all back to God. Ego rules the world of illusion, although it tries to trick us into believing that its chicanery is real and the spiritual path is nonsense. Ego receives for the self alone. If you love the ego, you can convert it to serve as a doorkeeper to higher consciousness," Swami imparted.

Kabbalah teaches that most of us live in the 1% unreal illusionary world, while the 99% real world is available to us. Maya is the 1%, and the Atman or Brahmin flourish in the 99% world.

"The ego I understand. Remembering the true character of my ego has heightened my awareness of how it lies to me," I offered.

"To guard against the ego is to be on guard against you, is it not true?" Swami said.

I nodded and continued.

"Lesson two is God or No God? Each of us must decide whether there is a God or not. If we say, "No God," we have to keep looking. God *is* within each of us as Vedanta teaches—God is the Brahmin or Atman. God is permissive and waits for me to come back to Him when I stray. God is not judgmental. Rather it is my separated-from-God self who judges me. God is that part of me longing to reconnect to others who are also on the path to finding Him within them," I stated.

"Swami, I have come to understand that a macrocosmic God watches over all of us, and a microcosmic God who is energetically connected to the Big God is within each of us. Do you agree, Swami?"

"Ramapriya, you always quote the scripture, '... and a child shall lead them ...' I believe I just heard that little Albert has led you to a concept of God that works for you.

"When you first came to me you said that a woman wanted you to sit on the beach with her in Maui. I said to stay where you were and to see God in others long enough and God would reach out and touch you. Has he touched you yet, Ramapriya? Are you consumed with a light to share with those who have lost their way?" he asked, staring into my eyes.

"I want to do God's will, not mine. You also said to get out of God's way." I leaned back onto the sofa.

"That is not what I said, Ramapriya, but you express yourself very well," he said as he smiled broadly.

"Lesson three, the light will never fail, lets me know that each of us is filled with the light of the Creator, no matter how dimly it shines. The light and love of God never die, but lie dormant within us. Our High Self connection can awaken the light by receiving that light to share, not for the self alone. It is never too late to return to God. Through this process of clearing—removing 'bread of shame'—we can reclaim our authentic selves," I said.

A famous Kabbalah tale addresses this lesson brilliantly. During the nine months we spend in our mother's womb, an angel holds a candle for us, teaching us the wisdom of the universe. We behold everything, from the beginning of the world to the end of the world. When we are born, the angel gives us a sharp blow on the upper lip and it makes us forget everything we have learned. Yet memory traces remain in our souls. The idea of God resonates with us, and upon these residual memories we build our consciousness.

"You have become less Albert and more who God created you to be. How did this happen?" he asked as he rang a bell for tea.

"I learned who I am by experiencing a lot of pain being who I am not. I have wanted what I wanted and not enough what God wanted for me. I can talk about how evil my ego self is, but more often than not I make choices that align me with the deceitfulness of my ego.

"Will I ever find favor in God's eyes?"

"Not if you constantly look. It is the same with God as with man. Find satisfaction within yourself. Love yourself and you will be as popular as the French baker at daybreak," Swami said.

Again my master smiled as his assistant poured tea.

"You are at lesson four, I believe. Continue," he said.

"Lesson four says that the family is the karmic mirror. What we have come back to Earth to learn is in the family circle. Seeing our parents as who they truly are—their good qualities as well as their character defects—exposes what we need to look at within ourselves. We are our parents. If you disapprove of a parent, it is because he or she has qualities that you had in a previous life. You have come back hypersensitive to these characteristics that your shadow transfers to your parents—so you can see them. The secret to wholeness is to see them mirrored so they can be corrected within you.

"We can change patterns of dysfunction in the family by exposing secrets and healing emotional pain. None of us is born into a family by accident. Everything has been prearranged. We pick a family whose karma fits our own.

"Some people see only the good in all of us and believe their parents are perfect. What would you say about them?" Swami asked.

"I think they are in denial."

"Perhaps," he advised.

"To my way of thinking, Earth is like a reform school where we make amends for past mistakes. You once told me that even a guru like you was far from perfect. As much as I like to see what's good in me or anyone else, I have to keep digging until I get to what drove me and them back here to the Lower World to face past misdeeds," I added.

"Everything I am learning is tied to paradox. It is all about me—looking at my part in what went wrong in all areas of my life instead of blaming others—but it is also all about all of us. Life is repertory theatre; each of us plays a part to teach and learn important lessons."

"Continue," Swami said.

"Lesson five is you're not who you think you are, and things are not what they seem. I woke up to the concept of the shadow and how it represents the spirit of the feminine within me and the masculine within women. This shadow or invisible partner is the one with whom I must make peace and come into balance in order to have healthy and loving relationships with all people, but especially with someone whom I love and with whom I want to spend my life."

"Gender is part mask, and without integration of the shadow, we will continue to live half a life. The Adam and Eve biblical fable represents how the split happened. Reconnecting to the light of the Creator, I can access historical memory that led to spiritual holism through gender assimilation.

"Parents, teachers, and peer groups have identified us through their own bias. Rather than being the son or daughter of our parents, we are the sons and daughters of God—macrocosmic and microcosmic—returning to Earth on assignment to clear up the past and to help others do the same. And it is only as a male united with my inner feminine personality that I can do what I came back to do.

"I am man and woman. My true partner is within me. For millennia and lifetimes I have been looking for a partner to make me happy, but I can only find joy within myself, and then, if it be God's will, I can have a partner outside myself.

"What appeared to be one thing was actually something else. I often believe that had I been smarter or more alert I could have avoided certain people or unpleasant circumstances. Now I know that these apparent negatives were teachers, and I experienced soul growth by working through to the light of the lessons. As a child, I did not like either of my parents. With time and spiritual soul growth, I have come to know that they were my greatest teachers.

"The ego created the separation between men and women. Fallen angels like you will bring them back together," Swami stated as he closed his eyes.

What I was gleaning from Swami was that there are no right answers. Shards of discovery without calendars and clocks lead us to illumination.

"All paths that lead to God are right paths," played in my head. It will always be a reminder of what drew me most strongly to Vedanta and Ramakrishna, my chosen ideal.

I drifted off.

Knowing that I am not who I think I am is freeing. I never felt like I belonged, whether at home, in my community, or at school, and rarely did I feel that friends and acquaintances were who they thought they were. I am becoming; I am unfolding, and I am remembering who I am.

When I am clear, meditation keeps me centered. I observe my deceptive ego like I would a person I don't trust. What's he up to? Where did that idea come from? What are the consequences if I listen to my dark side? When I obey my gut instincts I live in the will of my High Self.

I sat up with a start to find Swami drinking more tea.

"Was there another lesson you wished to discuss before we go to vespers?" he asked.

"I am ready for the evening service. My body and soul need to rest and relax," I answered.

Swami chuckled with me as we rose to go into the temple. As we walked alongside the rose garden, Swami picked a big, full-bloomed red rose and handed it to me.

"This reminds me of your newfound wisdom, Ramapriya. Let us put it on the altar tonight."

As soon as we were inside the temple, I sat straight back against the chair and floated off to that special place I go.

Lesson 6:

Forgiveness

Paul spoke.

Now Albert, you must face both the dark and light side of your-self. It is at this stage that you must look through the memory book of all the lives you've ever lived and all the harm and good you've ever done to others. It will be as your Bible says in 1 Corinthians 13:12:

> For now I see through a glass, darkly; but then
> face to face; now I know in part; but then shall
> I know even as I am known.

As your third eye opened when we first reconnected, to help you see where you had been and where you were going, those who you feel have done you wrong are your greatest teachers. Your dark side teaches you more than all the Sunday school stories you've ever heard. It is the dark night of the soul that connects you to your fellowman. Your separation brings you back to those who have fallen from grace with you.

Just as there is the God within, there is a macro-ego as well as a micro-ego. The macro-ego seduces people globally, influencing world leaders, politicians, actors, business tycoons, athletes, and many others who are susceptible to the lures of fame and fortune. Because the world overvalues celebrities and treats them like royalty, these exalted people put the masses under a spell—a hypnotic trance state—to shape the way you think, how you act, what you wear, and the lengths to which you will go to vicariously touch the lives of fame.

I checked in with myself to review what Paul was saying. His words were foreshadowing the most difficult lesson I needed to learn: forgiveness. I cannot fake how I feel toward those who have harmed me. I cannot ignore the good I have done, or the good in others. To be free of the bondage of self and others, I must heal resentments. I sensed that I must look at my enemies and express my anger and rage

Rage is a gargantuan part of forgiveness. I suggest that you make a list of all the people you have harmed and another list of all the people who have harmed you. Write them the nastiest, meanest epistle you can conceive. That's what I did, and it worked. I still use this exercise to heal relationships with those I find unforgivable. Go deep into repressed rage pockets and come up with some real barnburner pot shots. Let 'em have it. No holds barred. Don't mail the letter, and never lay someone low with angry confrontation. Talk these feelings over with a counselor, someone you trust.

Expressing your anger and rage is a precursor to being able to get to the mother lode of love and forgiveness. All forgiveness is about forgiving yourself—no matter what the circumstances and no matter who did what to whom.

The first name on my list of people who did me the most harm was me. I had to face how I had been the father of all my shame, disappointments, and unfinished business with God—how He created me to be one person, and I was determined to be someone else. It was only with guidance from the ego that I got to fail at the life I thought I was supposed to live. The ego helped me destroy the false self with alcoholic behavior. This was how my dark side had colluded with my light, to help me find the real me under the rubble of my inauthentic self.

To realize that all misdeeds were mine but not committed by the authentic me brought me little solace. I liken karmic debts to a crime scene. Even though I knew the real me was blameless, that it was my ego leading me down the primrose path to wrong choices, my fingerprints were on all my misdeeds. If I could somehow, with astute guidance from a counselor or mentor, inventory my life and see where I went wrong, I could make amends to those I had harmed and ultimately forgive myself.

I dared not shortchange this process. I had to face all of my transgressions and ask forgiveness of myself and those I had harmed. Buried deeply and oftentimes forgotten were shameful things that I had done or that others had done to me—which became secrets that I would not share under penalty of death. They had to be dredged up and exposed in order to heal.

Not all amends would be received with a kind and loving "thank you and God bless you." Several years ago, I went to someone I had harmed to ask his forgiveness. He was the last person on Earth to whom I wanted to humble myself. When I was finished with my amends, he started in on me. This man told me that I was sneaky, irresponsible, and untrustworthy. He kept me in my seat for four hours—I was in his house—while he unloaded every unrequited emotion he had about his wife and parents and all his friends and enemies. It was not easy, and I think I slept for twenty-four hours after taking leave of his ranting. But I was free from him and my transgressions, because I got honest with myself and sought forgiveness from him.

The banker was somewhat the same story. I gave an Oscar-worthy explanation—meek mixed with down-and-out in Sedona—why I had not paid on my credit card. I threw in the part about going to meetings and doing step work with my sponsor, and he said with a stone face, "If you're through with your cocka-mamie story, show me the money."

I saw a restaurateur whom I had stiffed for several thousand dollars. He was drinking too much the night that I ran into him, but when I approached him he asked about me and how I was.

I said to him, "Jerry, I owe you money, and I want to make financial amends."

"Albert, I know to the penny how much you owe my restaurant. You're sober—obviously I'm not—so take the money you owe me and help someone else trying to get sober. When someone needs something to eat, feed him. When a homeless man or woman stumbles into a meeting, give them shelter. Good luck to you. You came to me like a man, humbled yourself, and I respect that."

He turned and went back to his friends, but I have kept my end of the bargain through the years. Since that night I have repaid my debt as he asked me to do. It sounds saccharine to say, but Jerry was quoting scripture: "For I was hungry, and ye gave me meat: I was thirsty, and ye gave me drink: I was a stranger, and ye took me in …."

Making amends is not about the response you get, but how free you will be. Most people to whom you make amends are going to find you courageous and humble to seek forgiveness for what you have done. But don't count on it. Make amends for yourself. Oh, and one other thing, forgiving someone does not insinuate approval of him or his behavior. As we say in sober rooms, when a thief gets sober, you have a sober thief.

The caterpillar crawls into the cocoon and emerges a butterfly. Your ego must go through a similar conversion. The ego must humble itself to God, die, and resurrect. The ego at one moment is the nefarious, deceitful, dishonest, dark part of you, and when you surrender and die to your false self, you are reborn a precious child of God. But you need to reaffirm your God-self daily because it often shape shifts back to the ego self.

Forgiving yourself is a prerequisite to forgiving others. God may be all-seeing and all-knowing, but He wants you to come to Him and admit your wrongdoing as a right step to redemption. When you make amends, it makes your life cleaner, clearer, and better. To ask for forgiveness shows a desire to reclaim your birthright and be the legitimate you, who always was and always will be.

When you face the truth looking back at you from the karmic mirror, those who have harmed you are mere reflections of what you've done to hurt others. The more you forgive, the closer you come to who you really are. Never say "I am sorry" or "I apologize." Rather say, "I want to make amends for what I have done to harm you. "I am sorry" and "I apologize" are passive-aggressive ploys that a lot of us use to get the heat off of us—and they are meaningless words—and don't clear the slate. Amends identify you as authentic and begin to separate you from the ego-driven self who harmed others.

Unless you make amends to those you have harmed, you will be tied to them forever. Your ex-husband will show up in every man you meet, because you never cleaned up the wreckage of your marriage. Refuse to ask your mother for forgiveness, and she will express herself in every new woman who comes into your life.

Selfishness and self-seeking will fade and vanish. Remorse, self-pity, and feelings that no one loves you will melt under the lights of love and forgiveness.

"Let us rise." The voice of Swami wafted through my sluggish consciousness as I was returning to ground zero.

Amrita hurried out, as there were several of us guests for dinner.

I sat with several monks and another devotee from San Francisco, a man eager to leave the business world and seek solace here in the Vedanta Society. His story sounded too close to mine. I kept quiet. Listening is an art form far more endangered than talking.

"Albert, learn to listen, and listen to learn," my sobriety sponsor Fil used to say to me when I was getting sober.

After the meal, a tall, thin, bearded disciple came out of the kitchen carrying a five-tiered chocolate cake. Amrita gasped.

"Oh, my God. Albe—I mean Ramapriya's cake! Where did it come from? Ramapriya, you came with nothing today. Here's the cake," she said, flustered and excited to be eating the famous Hamburger Hamlet cake.

"It's either a miracle or somebody's copied the Hamlet's chocolate cake recipe," I said and shrugged.

"It is not important where the cake came from. It is gratifying that we can have as much chocolate as we like," Swami answered.

We all ate and drank tea or coffee and talked into the night. One of the monks came and told me that Swami had asked that I stay the night, as I had been working hard to explain my concept of spiritual lessons to him all afternoon.

My room was spartan, with a bed, a table, a chair, a lamp, and a tiny bathroom. There were two Vedanta books by Swami Vivekananda and Swami Swahananda. I read until I was sleepy.

As I drifted off to sleep, I heard Paul's voice as I went deeper: **Forgive.**

Chapter 9

Brother's Keeper

Several months passed with no new lessons or spiritual revelations. I began to sense a change in my perception of whom I was and what I was doing. Clients bothered me less. I dealt with them with patience and genuine tolerance.

My attitude altered toward my mother; I loved her more. Maggie didn't know me, so I felt she couldn't love me. That changed. I no longer saw her sacrifices as martyrdom. My judgments and criticisms changed into pride for what she had done. I admired her ability to raise six children as a single parent, and how she continued to care for her neighbors after her retirement. Mother shopped for their groceries, ran errands, did minor bookkeeping, and sat and read to them and comforted their families when they died.

Mother sent me a stack of poetry that she had written over a thirty-year period. My good friend Martha Orr White edited the poems, and I published *Poems That My Mother Wrote* in 1992. Her minister read this selection at her funeral:

Lord, let me live until spring
When flowers bloom, birds sing,
Trees begin to bud, turn green;
To feel warmth on my back.
O Lord, let me live until spring.

And live until spring she did. Mother died on March 23, 1996. In retrospect, I suspect that she knew she was able to see the future, that she was aware that we choose when to be reborn and when to die.

I became amused when I heard what someone thought of me. Not taking myself so seriously and learning to laugh at myself helped immensely. Client complaints became open doors to how I could serve them. I quit burying moods like a dog would a bone and became more forthcoming, more willing to clear misunderstandings. I tracked my ego cautiously but with stubborn determination.

When I projected some quality or characteristic, I discussed my transference with the person involved. I was able to understand the difference between what the ego demanded and what High Self guidance suggested.

Did my life become perfect? It did not. Did it get a lot better? It did, because I was a lot clearer. I focused on spiritual lessons in meditation, and truth walked in just like Paul had done that first afternoon in Birmingham. Like one trying to become accomplished at the piano, I practiced what I had been given.

The clearer I became, the more I accepted who I was, and the fewer expectations I had of myself and others. I woke most days waiting for what God wanted me to have and to do.

I continued to travel to see clients. In mid-May of 1989, I treated myself to ten days at Sheila Cluff's Oaks at Ojai, a reasonably priced spa at a quaint inn twenty miles from the Pacific Ocean, near Ventura, California. Hikes and stretching, aerobics and weight classes, and the most delicious low-fat 1,000 calories a day from master chef Eleanor Brown are the reasons I go back year after year. I needed the Oaks desperately after four days of self-indulgence at Los Angeles's swan-lake-floral-paradise Hotel Bel-Air.

I got back to Sedona eight pounds lighter, and in time to greet all the tourists who crawled up the hill from Phoenix for Memorial Day weekend. Since I had not seen my friend Russ Moker in months, we decided to have brunch at Cups Bistro on West Highway 89A.

After the Oaks at Ojai, my resolution was to avoid fatty foods. Cups had a large refrigerator case with desserts made with fudge, peanut butter, and butterscotch filling. I spied a fruit tart that fit my diet, so I bought it.

Cups Bistro had tiny café tables, making it hard for two people to sit and drink and eat at the same table. But we did it. Many times four or five people sat and drank and dunked and schmoozed.

As I sat down, a voice from the dessert display said, "Let me know if you like that fruit tart."

I took a bite and said, "No fat, not fried, no sugar … no taste. Try it. Not bad."

Two couples sat opposite Russ and me. One of the four was the man who had asked me about the tart. He was of average height, blond haired, with piercing hazel eyes.

Our eyes locked. There was a moment of recognition.

"I saw your picture in the paper today," I said to him.

"What paper?" he asked.

"USA Today," I replied.

"What was I doing?" he wanted to know.

"You were jogging with the president of the United States," I responded.

"I am amazed that you recognized me. I was running with the president and ten other SEALs with my head down. How did you spot me?" he asked.

I shrugged with an "I don't know" look on my face.

"I'm Victor Meyer. This is my wife, Lisa, and my brother David and his friend Linda."

We all shook hands. Russ introduced himself and then said, "Don't ever ask how Albert knows anything. Knowing what the rest of us don't is his business."

I had a personal training session in ten minutes. I rose to leave.

"Victor, if you'd like to work out at Los Abrigados Sedona Health Spa, I'll have passes for you at the desk. Get the directions from Russ," I said.

Victor apparently worked out a lot. He was robust, tanned, and very healthy looking. I had the feeling I "knew" him.

On Monday when I came back into the spa, Victor had left his name and address for me. Within a few days, notes crossed in the mail. I sent him a letter describing why he seemed intuitively familiar to me. Victor sent me a French picture postcard of a child with the words *Tu es mon ami,* you are my friend. I have always felt that I lived in France around the time of the French Revolution. I am very drawn to the Napoleonic period, and years ago I hung a large John Dawson oil painting of Napoleon in my living room.

One late September day, I got a telephone call from Victor. He would be driving through Sedona in a few days and wanted to know if he could stop by. The French Navy had accepted him into its two-year exchange SEAL program. He would be stationed near Marseilles in the south of France.

At 5:30 on a Sunday afternoon, the doorbell rang. I opened the door and there stood Victor.

"Come in," I said cordially, shaking his hand and helping with his garment bag.

He looked at me with those intense eyes and said stoically, "What am I doing here, and why do you have a portrait painting of Napoleon on that wall?"

Victor's question precipitated hours of discussion about reincarnation, why certain people are brought back together, and what the reunion is all about. "You pick right back up where you left off," I said. "Sometimes it's just to say 'Hello, good-bye,' and at other times you have to complete unfinished business."

We joked for awhile about which one of us had been Napoleon. Truth be told, he and I were together in that historical period. I also got intuitive flashes that we had been in the Vatican together and in the dynasty of Ramses II in Egypt.

He said that he had been raised a Baptist, and that Baptists don't believe in reincarnation. "Unfortunately, I, too, was a Baptist until I left divinity school at nineteen. Thank God I found booze instead of the ministry," I said, watching his reaction.

We dined at the Heartline Café, one of Sedona's best restaurants. The beautiful gardens provide not only fragrant flowers and shrubs with an Italian water fountain, but a quieter spot to have a decent conversation.

"I found your letter about our previous lives in Italy, Egypt, and especially France very fascinating, as I am about to live in the south of France for two years. How do you know we have been together?" Victor asked.

"I just know it. My intuition tells me that we synchronistically met that morning at Cups Bistro because we have unfinished business. We made a date telepathically to be there on the same day and at the same time. The minute I saw you, felt your energy, I knew that I knew you. When you spoke, the sound of your voice confirmed it," I said.

"Some of your ideas are strange, Albert, but I am very attracted to what you have to say, for a couple of reasons. First, you're so positive and energetic with how you say things. And secondly,

I do feel this powerful energy exchange. How do you know it's a past-life connection?" Victor asked.

"I don't know. You just have to trust your gut instinct. Intuition is the wavelength of recognition. Give it time. Soon you will know if our reunion is going to be for mutual benefit or if we have unpleasant karmic situations to work through.

"If you owe me any pounds from Egypt or francs from France, I'll send the bill collector around to see you for my money," I joshed. Victor playfully jabbed my arm.

Phyllis and Chuck Cline own the Heartline Café and always send complimentary desserts to my table. Tonight it was a platter of peach yogurt, flourless chocolate cake, coconut cake, and fresh fruit. We both dove in as if we had the metabolism of Olympians. He did, but I didn't.

"This is interesting, but how could Christians and Catholics have been so wrong about reincarnation? They flatly deny it exists," Victor said, eating the last of the flourless chocolate cake.

"You forgot the Jews. The Kabbalah and the Zohar teach that all of us reincarnate to refine the soul. The church, like the state, doesn't want to lose control over its members (or constituencies), so it disavows any information that doesn't affirm what it wants us to believe. It's about control rather than what is true," I said. "Jewish mysticism says that not only must you live life after life, but that your astrology birth chart is the roadmap for your life. Your birth chart points out your positive qualities and negative traits, what you need to atone for, what opportunities exist for you, and when these growth challenges will appear in your life.

"A lot of information has come to light in the last fifty years— the Dead Sea scrolls, the Nag Hammadi library, and the Gospel of Judas among them—to expose the lies of Christianity, and I mean all churches … Baptist, Episcopal, Unity, the Catholic church, and many other sects. When the planet Pluto goes into

Capricorn in 2008, there is a strong possibility that chaos will arise within organized religions," I said.

"I am very drawn to everything you say, but I have been raised to believe another way. Your points of view are strange on the one hand, but very appealing to me on another," Victor said calmly.

"As a young boy, I was taught a lot of things that never made sense. I went to church. I sang songs. I was baptized. I loved the music, but the sermons never clicked with me. No matter how loud the preacher preached, no matter what he said, my still, small voice of intuition whispered, 'It's not true.' It would say, 'Keep looking.'"

"Albert, you are so darned passionate about things. Where does all this enthusiasm come from?" Victor asked.

"Pain and suffering. I tried to be someone I wasn't, and it nearly killed me. I took a death-spiral to rock bottom through booze and bad credit. I had to get out of where I was, no matter what price I had to pay. I have learned how to live by never wanting to live the way I lived before. I have found a God of my own understanding, not a bushel of bastardized Bible-thumping guilt trips. When I played out the scene of running, hiding, and living in shame, I cleaned up the wreckage of my past and let God run the show. I made amends and never looked back."

It was time for a lighter note. Victor struck one with his innocence and candor. "Don't you find it interesting that I am a Baptist United States Navy SEAL search-and-destroyer, and you are a fallen Baptist who doesn't believe in war? How did we ever find each other, and what are we supposed to do now that we are back together?" he wanted to know.

I nodded and shrugged but remained silent.

"I have two years in France. I'll remain open to all of this new information. Send me all the metaphysical books you want me to read. I'll use your meditation tapes and keep a journal. As a matter of fact, why don't you come to Paris for Thanksgiving?" Victor asked.

"I'll come, but I pick the hotel. I have a suspicion that the government still believes you can see Paris on five dollars a day."

As we were paying the bill, Victor pulled at my arm and said, "You want to hear a strange coincidence? Your telephone number was my military number at the United States Naval Academy."

I am accustomed to synchronicities, gut reactions, click connections, intuitions, and miraculous signs, but it still takes me by surprise when one comes along. That's the kid in me. I never want to get so big for my britches that I don't get a thrill when I see one of God's flash cards.

I recognized Victor from a picture in the newspaper. What are the odds? We both have a passion for France—her cuisine and museums, her people and the French Revolution, as well as Napoleon. His military number being the same as my telephone number cinched it for me. Meeting Victor Meyer was a God shot.

The weeks before I met Victor in France flew by with client consultations by telephone and in Sedona and work trips to major cities like Los Angeles, Dallas, New York, Chicago, and Birmingham. I lectured and held seminars with curious folks looking for answers to life's problems. My attitude toward being an astrologer was changing. Swami's words, "see God in someone long enough and one day God will reach out and touch you," went with me everywhere.

I booked rooms in Paris at Le Grand Hotel Inter-Continental across from the Opera House. The Grand Hotel is a majestic eighteenth-century building with a marble staircase, high vaulted ceilings, and elaborate cornices and moldings. Good imitation antique furniture, expensive oil paintings, and Persian rugs filled the reception area and the lobby and its spacious, winding foyers and sitting rooms.

I slept all morning and afternoon. Every hour I would awaken, attempt to get up, and then fall back exhausted into bed. At about six o'clock, the phone rang. It was Victor. He had just arrived on the express train from Toulon. I told him he had a room next to mine, to check in at the reception desk, and then come by and we'd go to dinner.

Victor reported that he had a full schedule for our four-day holiday.

"Tomorrow I thought we would go to Versailles, if you would like to see the grand palace of Louis XIV," Victor said.

I was impressed at how much thought he had given to our Thanksgiving holiday. When I took a course in the French Revolution in college, Professor Wiley underscored how we must one day come to France.

"I'd love to see Versailles. Where do we go after that, my Francophile?"

"I know you like art. Tomorrow afternoon we will go to the Barnes Collection at the Musée D'Orsay. The next day we will take in the Louvre."

We left the hotel to explore. It was cold and damp, typical Paris weather for late November. Although Victor and I were new friends, our conversations were what you would expect from lifelong pals. He would speak and I would finish his sentence. I would say something and he said he was thinking the same thing at the same time. We were in synch.

"Victor, do you know Les Deux Magots Café? It is quite popular with artists and writers. How about a light supper before we go back to the hotel?"

He indicated that he hung out there all the time, so we jumped into a taxi and headed for the Left Bank. The clock struck eleven as we arrived. It was crowded and smoky. There was no magic, just stale tobacco air—everyone in Paris seems to chain-smoke—and loud-mouthed drunks. So this was one of Hemingway's haunts, I thought to myself. Today it was a tourist trap—overpriced food that tasted not so good.

Service was slow. It was hard to eat while bathed in nicotine ozone. After an interminable time, we at last stepped outside into a drizzling rain. No taxis. I looked across and saw a church. The door was open. A few stragglers went in and came out.

"What church is that, Victor, do you know?"

"It is St-Germain-des-Prés. The church has a very interesting history. I'm reading about Comte Saint Germain in one of those books you sent from the Golden Word Bookstore in Sedona," he said proudly.

It is believed that Saint Germain was born in 1561. Legend has it that he was a master alchemist and was able to make himself invisible. He was known as "the man who never dies and knows everything."

St-Germain-des-Prés is the oldest church in Paris. It was built by the Merovingian King Childebert in 542 to house holy relics. It was rebuilt during the 11th century, the 19th century, and again in the 1990s. Since its inception, it was a very influential Benedictine abbey. During the French Revolution, it burned.

"Let's go in for a minute since we can't get a cab," I suggested.

We ran across the street and into this very dark and Gothic cathedral. A host of angels appeared to hover and float near the ceiling. My imagination ran amok. There was no question that something was astir here. I have a well-honed intuition as well as a vivid imagination. It must be the smoke-cloud from all these candles burning, I thought, as my mind tried to reassure me.

There were the usual icons and relics. Candles blazed from wall sconces, and chanting echoed around the church. Congregants filled the pews in the middle of the church and the benches near the altar.

We have a similar sanctuary in Sedona, the Chapel of the Holy Cross. For a donation, people are encouraged to light candles for the welfare of themselves and others. The practice was prevalent here, as worshippers lit candles and prayed.

Victor and I went to different parts of the church. I was drawn to the altar. Winter-bright flowers cascaded over the entry to the front of the cathedral. Rose-scented candles burned in heavy matte-green gold candelabra. I sat down on the front pew and fell into a swoon I know so well. I heard nothing but the thunder of silence.

Lesson 7:

You Are Your Brother's Keeper

Albert, you have been climbing Jacob's ladder. You are at a stage of your journey, remembering a lesson that leads to your redemption. But it requires that you come back with a brother or sister. You have selected Victor, an old friend from many lifetimes, to make the journey with you.

You two have met again so that he can be opened from within himself and to access his storehouse of memories and Gnostic truths. He speaks about a lot of things that are not his ideas or his beliefs. Victor will trust the process as he begins to embrace his authentic self. He will change in his time. Do not judge a book by its cover. Watch how he transforms. Continue to use fairy tales and star power to help him as he unfolds. Ali Baba said to the cave, "Open, sesame," and it did. It will be the same with Victor. You have come back to give him his code.

He will meet and marry a woman from France within two years. They will have two children, a boy and a girl.

It is his fate to be a householder, to work through selfishness and arrogance with his wife and to guide his children to be as they were born to be.

You remembered compassion and service to others at an early age. Remember Blanche?

Blanche ironed for my family every Wednesday. Poor people in the forties couldn't afford automobiles, so she rode the streetcar from the ghetto to our apartment in Elyton Village, a federally funded public-housing development in Birmingham, Alabama, known as the projects. Back then, my family used public transportation for the same reason Blanche did. We were poor and had no alternative.

One day as she was coming to work on the streetcar, the driver shut the door before Blanche could board. She fell into the street and broke her foot. This was Alabama in the forties. This was the South before Rosa Parks and Martin Luther King changed civil rights for Negroes forever. The bus driver did not stop to see if she was injured; he drove on.

I was fuming mad as a nine-year-old that Blanche had been hurt by the carelessness of a streetcar driver and decided to do something about her injury. I went with her to city hall to file a report and to seek compensation for her medical bills. Although we got the runaround and went through mounds of red tape, we persevered. Blanche was reimbursed for her broken foot and for the carelessness of the streetcar driver. She did not get what she deserved, but she won against great odds in a political climate that was not used to being fair and balanced with blacks.

I did not hesitate a minute before I decided to take on city hall with Blanche. She was my best friend, and I loved her. Blanche taught me about love and caring; I taught city hall not to mess with my Blanche.

Paul, but what about those who suffer from injustice, who are hungry and naked? What about men and women and children who speak a different language, worship in a mosque, and whose lives my government is destroying? Do I raise my voice against these atrocities? Do I vote my conscience of care and concern? Do I dare risk losing my comfort zone for the sake of being my brother's keeper halfway around the world, or next door?

You are doing what you resonate to do. You reach out when you see a need. All of you are in this drama of transformation together, even those who have not awakened to the challenge.

Kay Warren, wife of Rick Warren, who wrote *The Purpose-driven Life,* is executive director of the HIV/AIDS initiative at

Saddleback Church in Lake Forest, California. She recently wrote an e-commentary for CNN, entitled "Christians must do more to combat AIDS, comfort victims."

She recorded an account of an African woman named Joana, emaciated with AIDS, who greeted her when Kay toured Mozambique. Joana had unrelenting diarrhea, little food, no earthly possessions, and only an elderly aunt who had taken pity on her to care for her needs. A short time later Joana died—rejected, abandoned, persecuted, and destitute. Warren writes, "I had no medication that could cure Joana, nothing to alleviate her pain, nothing that would restore her to health. But I offered her the one thing that all of us can offer: I offered my presence. I put my arms gently around her, prayed for relief from her suffering and whispered, 'I love you.'"

This is the lesson of "brother's keeper" in practice. This is the lesson that whenever anyone anywhere needs my help, I want to be able to reach out and give assistance. This is the Golden Rule, and this is what Christ and Buddha and Krishna taught us about how to treat others.

Captain Scott Southworth was serving in the U.S. Army in Iraq in 2003 when a three-year-old boy with cerebral palsy named Allah crawled across the floor of the orphanage to Scott where he was volunteering. When Scott returned to the United States, he could not get Allah out of his mind. Something inside of him spoke to Scott about wanting to take care of this boy, to be his father. Against the greatest odds, and with the cooperation of the U.S. Embassy in Iraq, Scott, who was not married, adopted Allah.

Several years ago, a minister in Chicago suggested to me and my business partner Scott that we ask people we meet every day, "What can I do for you?" No matter how dire your circumstances or how needy you are, ask the people you meet, "What can I do for you?" Try it. You will be shell shocked to note how many people have never been asked if someone can help them. If you want to know who your brothers and sisters are, ask the question, "What can I do for you?" Ask that question even if you think you need help, that you have nothing to give.

Has someone who needs your help crossed your path? Did you leave it to someone else to lend a helping hand, or did you offer your support or your resources? Would you have been open to helping a young boy with a handicap from which he will never recover? Are you open to the still, small voice of God when He asks you to be your brother's keeper?

The Lord asks, "Where is your brother?" In our world of abject materialism, who will feed and clothe your brother if you don't? When you see the homeless, do you look the other way or think that street people have brought their condition on themselves?

Actor George Clooney doesn't. He calls upon the haves to feed the have-nots, our brothers and sisters in the Sudan. President Bill Clinton teamed up with international rock star and goodwill ambassador Bono from the band U2 to ask for our help to find a cure for AIDS in Africa and other epidemic centers in the world. For some, the help is financial assistance, while for others it is to raise the awareness of this dreaded disease. Actor Susan Sarandon takes to the streets to try to stop genocide in Iraq because she is her brother's keeper; she is a guardian at the gate of decency and humanity. Do you want to emulate Susan? Ask as Christ did, "Where is my brother?" Billionaire Warren Buffet recently gave Bill Gates' foundation thirty-five billion dollars to give away to causes that need money to help a lot of brother and sisters.

Are we our brother's keeper? Yes we are, and it is time that we realize that our brother may be next door, but he is also thousands of miles away. Apathy perpetuates starvation, and it allows wars to continue to be waged.

In Paris I knew that I was in a place where I had lived many times before. I would experience both pleasant memories and painful ones as I continued my soul journey. Victor and I had been together many times. When he came back into my life, I felt no doubt that I had to help him remember his truth rather than stay blocked by dogma. He was searching for answers. I would help him find them where the questions were, within him.

Victor was a trained killer, and I was a pacifist; I had never handled a gun—I favored gun control. He was a traditional Christian, and I was a man of many faiths. He stood ready to carry out the orders of the military, and I stood ready to dismantle his military orders to invade and harm civilians in a country that is not ours to occupy.

Where is your brother, Albert? Are you your brother's keeper even if he does not share your beliefs? Can you 'love thy neighbor as thyself?' Can you lead by example and let what you do speak louder than what you say? Can you love someone who is not lovable? Can you practice patience and nonjudgment to help your brother—the one God drew to you with the magnetism of compassion and concern?

When we met, the resonance of Victor's voice drew me to him. I heard him before I saw him. The moment he heard me speak, he listened and he was affected. Although our beliefs were different, our memory books of shared lives canceled out the differences. He learned from me and I from him. Difficulties would only arise when our wills would clash and our egos would deceive. I had to stay the course. I felt that my commission was to bring him to the light.

In past lives, he had been my student, my son, a friend, a brother. France is a karmic place for him and me. We both lived our last incarnation here, and it was here that we had to return to reactivate why we reunited.

I looked up and saw a painting of Saint Francis of Assisi. He was traveling by foot with his brother, a companion and fellow seeker. These men were committed to one another through God.

Saint Francis required brothers to go out in twos, because the road was less lonely and the work less tedious. Companionship—brotherhood—is crucial to man's successful return to God.

Victor, like I, had assumed a false identity through his karmic bloodline. He was carrying historical memory of a father's and grandfather's transgressions. Victor would clear these issues and become who he really was as I let him know how I freed myself of family karma. This was as it had to be: when someone has a need for help which we can give, it is our assignment to give it.

As man is both dark and light and all are created by and of God, when one returns to God, he must bring with him one in need of redemption. It is not enough to surrender to the error of one's former actions and deeds in this and former lives. You must be willing to lead another to the route back to God.

Within all is the light. The light may dim, and you may feel that God is dead. It is not true. As long as someone is there to lead the way, the lost one may return to the path.

A longtime friend Joseph Braswell called recently to tell me that he loved me. Joseph was diagnosed with pancreatic cancer this winter and chose not to go through chemotherapy. The voice within told me to write Joseph a note every week, which I did, and to make brief phone calls to him.

When we talked we spoke about the great adventure that lay ahead of him and how the soul continues when the body dies. He thanked me for not patronizing him about finding a miracle cure, but rather for supporting his decision to move forward rather than go to any lengths to prolong his life. Oftentimes we laughed out loud about some of the silly things we had done and also about how seriously he had always taken himself.

Joseph told me one night that we were soul brothers, because he cared for me as much as I cared for him, and that we had helped one another along the spiritual path. Joseph lived in New York for fifty years and was the first person to tell me about Marianne

Williamson, who is a compassionate and brilliant arbiter of where we humans are on the spiritual hierarchy. She certainly helped him prepare to leave his egocentric pleasure-bound self behind.

When Joseph died, he was looking ahead, not behind him. He is now enjoying his great adventure called life after life.

Continue to still your mind. Go always deep within yourself, where God is. Seek unattached, detached love. Pray without ceasing that God's will, not thy will, be done.

Slow down. Look back and see who falters and falls when his heart wants to go home. Reach out and pull the one who stumbles nearer to you.

See God in everyone. You are your brother's keeper.

I felt a nudge on my shoulder, and I opened my eyes and looked into the face of overpowering light, fixing my gaze on an angel.

"Albert, the church is about to close. I wondered where you were. I saw smoky haze and blinding light at the front of the cathedral. Are you all right?"

"Victor, you have been nibbling around for an answer to why we met. Would it satisfy you to know that we are brothers?" I said as we both exited the church.

"Albert, if we are brothers, I'd love to know who our mother is. She must be a hundred and one years old," he exclaimed as he ran to hail a cab, laughing at the prospect of Brother Albert, Brother Victor.

We went to Versailles the next day, saw a lot of art, and ate delicious food in small restaurants. It rained every day. We trudged through puddles and drank espresso and ate croissants all over Paris. It was the best four days I can remember.

"When you say that you are your brother's keeper, Albert, what exactly does that mean?" Victor asked.

"I talk a lot about the Holy Grail, as do you. I have come to understand that the grail is really an answer to the questions, "Who am I? What am I to do with my life?" A brilliant answer to that question appears in *Cup of Destiny* by Trevor Ravenscroft: "You cannot come to the Grail but that you bring your brother." The Bible reminds us that we are our brother's keeper. Since all of us have fallen from grace, we must come back to God bringing someone who has also fallen from grace, our brother or sister. Coming back alone is receiving redemption for the self alone. We must share redemption to receive it," I said.

I had to leave early on a Sunday morning, and he had to take the fast train back to Toulon. "This has been one of the best vacations I have ever had," I said to Victor. "I cannot tell you how difficult and unrewarding traveling with someone ordinarily is under the best of circumstances—"

"Even when you get the best room in the palace," Victor said with great amusement.

"That too," I agreed. "But I have loved everything about this vacation. It was meant to be. Seeing Paris with you had purpose."

We talked a bit longer and said we would stay in touch. He expressed an interest in knowing more about what I do with clients.

I took a long soak in the tub, a perfect place to review the last four days. Something inside of me said that Victor and I would have more to talk about and would reconnect. Paris had been a new beginning. No matter how many times someone like Victor walks back into my life it still amazes me.

As I turned back the covers to get into bed, I found a package and a note on my pillow. And by the light of the tiny bedside lamp I read the note first:

Dear Albert,

I thank you for your love, your kindness, and your forthrightness. I'm having the time of my life. You are a teacher, a father, a friend, a brother.

Love,

Victor

I opened the package, and inside was a black hooded sweatshirt. A note was pinned to the shirt that said:

This is one of the sweatshirts I had made for students in my SEAL training class last month. I felt like giving you one. Wear it with pride.

Victor

I unfolded the sweatshirt and on the back was stenciled "My Brother's Keeper." This was yet another eerie but confirming sign that there are no accidents. Victor and I had reunited for a powerful purpose.

I switched off the lamp and lay in bed reminiscing about my time with Victor. I was overjoyed and filled with love. I left the balcony door open to enjoy the chill of the night air.

Before I went to sleep, I picked up a book of poetry I had brought with me. I first read this poem as a young boy, from *A Child's Garden of Verses* by Robert Louis Stevenson.

My Shadow

I have a little shadow that goes in and out with me,
And what can be the use of him is more than I can see.
He is very, very like me from the heels up to the head;
And I see him jump before me, when I jump into my bed.

II

The funniest thing about him is the way he likes to grow—
Not at all like proper children, which is always very slow;
For he shoots up taller like an India-rubber ball,
And sometimes gets so little that there's none of him at all.

III

He hasn't got a notion of how children ought to play,
And can only make a fool of me in every sort of way.
He stays so close beside me, he's a coward you can see;
I'd think shame to stick to nursie as that shadow sticks to me!

IV

One morning very early, before the sun was up,
I rose and found the shining dew on every buttercup;
But my lazy little shadow, like an errant sleepy-head,
Had stayed at home behind me and was fast asleep in bed.

Chapter 10

The Love Chapter

Lesson 8:

Love Is All There Is

I must have good karma, because I managed to get my favorite cottage at San Ysidro Ranch, even without reservations. It was late at night when I reached Montecito. My adrenaline was jacked up sky high, so sleep was impossible. I went down to the beach and walked for miles. Christmas tree lights blinked from all the beach houses. Carols drifted down to the oceanfront as I sauntered through the wet black sand. An alcove drew me in, and I sat back and closed my eyes. Intuitive thoughts ran through my mind.

I am feeling on top of the world. For once in my life, I am clean inside. Everything and everywhere I go, what comes to me is love, love, love. Man, I see so many different kinds of love: courtly love, erotic love, familial love, free love, platonic love, puppy love, religious love, romantic love, unrequited love ....

Then there is the love of God.

I had always wondered what I was living for and what my purpose was. What was revealed to me is that love is all there is.

It seemed that most of us had been trying to figure things out and reaching faulty conclusions. Let things be revealed, my voice of intuition whispered. The more I moved away from the consciousness of worldly desire, the more I experienced my connection with God. I felt better knowing who I was and being driven by purpose, rather than blind ambition. I heard over and over: "All there is is love," and "Love is all there is." These phrases played in my mind like Bach, with words by Krishnamurti.

The thirty-minute walk and quiet time settled my muddy thoughts and left me in a clear, cool spring. I came to the beach with butterflies and bees in my brain and returned to the cottage with a smooth-as-glass mind ready for deep sleep. Not a sound, a dream, or a nightmare … just deep and peaceful sleep.

I awoke as the cock was crowing, rested and energized. Walking out the French doors, I sat down to read the *Los Angeles Times*. A leaflet was wrapped around the newspaper that said, "Love Is in the Air." I am getting used to these meaningful coincidences.

The coast a few miles away was clear, and the San Ysidro Ranch was bathed in radiant sun shining in a baby-blue cloudless sky.

Outlook I, II, and III are white Cape Cod–like connected cottages, and each has its own entrance. In December, decorated trees serve as centerpieces in all the gardens, and holly wreaths adorn each cottage door.

After reading the paper, I booted up my laptop, and my fingers flew across the keyboard. Ideas nestled in unhurried sentences tumbled onto the computer screen.

I need a breakfast break, I thought, as the clock struck eleven bells. Birds chirped, and fragrances wafted from the blooming trees, shrubs, and flower beds as I worked. If love is—and all there is, is—love, then it must be here today in Montecito on a crisp, clear December Sabbath, I said to myself.

I watched as a couple finished a morning run and walked slowly up the entry drive on the road below. He placed his arm about her shoulder, they took a few steps, and then he kissed her gently on the lips.

"Good morning. What are you doing working on a beautiful day like this?" I looked up, and the man who had just kissed his lady friend was addressing me.

"I am trying to record some information before I lose it," I replied. "Did you ever have a good idea or compose a letter in your head, only to have it disappear because you didn't write it down?"

"I've always said that a great idea becomes so much a part of you that it refuses to leave, like a hungry dog or cat, until it's been fed," he said.

"Oh, a Will Rogers humorist," I retorted.

"What are you writing about?" he asked.

"Hungry cats and dogs," I replied, and we both laughed. "Actually I am trying to do an exposé on how our minds keep us convinced that we're someone we're not. Call it an attempt to free a man from the vise-grip of his ego," I said, hoping he would go in and shower or eat breakfast.

"Fiction or nonfiction?" he wouldn't stop.

"Truth is stranger than fiction. Nobody really writes fiction."

The shy blond woman joined him on the porch. She listened without joining the conversation.

"So, are you writing fiction or nonfiction?" He kept it up.

"Truth or consequences," I replied. "Before I dig myself a deeper hole, tell me about you."

"I'm Robert Graves, and this is my wife, Andrea. I am CEO of Monarch Pictures," he said. I got up and introduced myself.

"I'd like to flatter myself and think that I am writing to help somebody like you two trust yourselves more. I would hope that you would take an inventory and change to be who you are, as opposed to who people think you are. Do I sound like one of those awful Bible thumpers doing a touchy-feely infomercial?"

"No, you sound like someone who's passionate about what he's doing. I like that in a person."

I was comfortable with Robert and Andrea Graves. They were genuine, open, and aware, and they wanted to connect with someone they didn't know to hear what he had to say.

"Robert, just saying it like it is is one of my gifts or curses. Pain got me to write. And inspiration provided the message. In addition to writing and lecturing, I work as a therapist with clients who want to get out of where they are. Alcohol, drugs, a cul-de-sac job, divorce, sexual issues, fear, rage, and depression drive people to change. You might say I am an in-your-face kind of therapist."

Just as the talk started, we all three got quiet and I went on writing. I liked this couple. They did not take themselves too seriously, especially him.

"Would you like to come over for coffee?" Andrea asked, sticking her head around the corner of her cottage.

"I'd love to," I answered, getting up and walking around to their side of the porch. She poured. They wanted to know if I cared for breakfast. I declined. I hadn't just lost thirty pounds to find them again in croissants or bagels and cream cheese.

Robert told me that he had been chairman of the board of a major utilities conglomerate when the owners of the studio wanted to move into twenty-first-century technology. Hence electrical power got into bed with star power.

"I thought you were in show business when we first met," Robert said.

"We're all in show business, Robert," I said, adding a new wrinkle to our conversation.

"Do you find it strange or unusual that some of us say the same things, Robert? And whose idea was it to invite me to coffee?" I asked.

"No, I feel that a lot of us are saying the same things in different ways. I knew the minute we met an hour ago that I wanted to know you. I asked Andrea to invite you."

"I knew the minute we met an hour ago that we knew each other from somewhere. Do you think it could have been in another life?" (I paused to see if they were giving me an Albert's-one-of-those-kind-of-guys look—they weren't. I continued.) "Actually, I was happy to talk with you, because you are what I am writing about today: Love is all there is," I said.

"Robert and I like how open you are. We are transplants from New Jersey, now living in Brentwood. Where do you live?" Andrea inquired.

"Sedona, Arizona."

"We have heard how beautiful it is but have never been there," Robert piped in.

"The book I'm writing is about how spiritual lessons can help you clear the patina from a masterpiece."

"It must take guts to confront somebody about their drinking," Robert stated.

"Not as much as it does to confront someone about his sexuality," I responded. "A man's feminine self is his creative side. It is the woman within the man that allows him to love. Man does not know how to love," I stated, and waited to see what damage the declaration did.

"Robert, this is so spooky. It's as if Albert has been listening to us talk for months," Andrea said with excitement.

"Andrea, we have all been saying this in our heads for centuries. Man is sick and tired of having to wrap his feelings in gym sweats. All this gender identity is what makes for suicides, alcoholism, drug addiction, divorce, and deep depression," I said.

"You know how to reduce the argument to bare bone," Robert said.

"Let's do shorthand, friends. You can either take a deep, scary look and change what you don't like, or live in denial and die of a bad attitude or stomach cancer." I said with the dramatic delivery of the actor in me.

"God, Albert, all we asked was 'what are you writing,'" Robert said, and we laughed together.

"We were going to go for a swim. That can wait. You have us stirred up in a way that we haven't been in years. How do you do it?" Andrea asked.

"Honey, I have no other choice but to be as I am. I paid a big price to think like I do. For twenty years, it took booze. Now it takes truth and a power source deep within me."

"Here we are, three people who just happened to meet at a fancy resort because they just happened to be assigned adjoining cottages," Andrea spoke up.

"There is no just-happened-to-meet about it. Everything is by divine design. Robert, you worked in the power and light industry. You didn't just happen to splice wires to get energy into the homes. There is a circuitry board with cables and wires precisely connected to permit transmission of light waves. The spiritual lessons upon which we rebuild our lives come to us by invisible wires—through quantum physics. Everything is energy.

"Watching you at a distance two hours ago was the perfect ending to the play I wrote myself into today. There was no high drama, no lightning strikes, and no thunderclap aria. It was just the two of you holding hands and then you embraced and kissed. It freed me that the road ended in love. I really feel like I have been a lucky man today to meet a man and a woman who showed me love.

"And in closing, the preacher said, all there is is love." I finished with a flourish, stood up, and took a deep bow. "The only promise I hear from my guidance is that if you take the road home one degree at a time and one lesson at a time, all there is is love."

We three stood quietly for a moment, embracing the new friendship and truth that inevitably emerge when courage speaks up.

Robert and Andrea had afternoon plans, and I needed to get back to writing. Before we said our good-byes, they asked me to go to a children's Christmas cantata at a local church that night. Without hesitation, I accepted. I went back to my side of the cottage to plug away. The weather was breezy but sunny, with blue skies all afternoon.

All there is is love.

Love is a song that lifts the human spirit. Love is the hand of hope. It is the first bud of spring. Love is a rainbow after the rain. And it is a painting by an artist. Love is all these things. You cannot wish for a bouquet of flowers and have them appear. A flower begins with a seed; add sunshine and rain, and in time the bloom appears.

For all there is is love.

One voice with the perfect harmonics can change the world. You can make a difference if you speak from the clear and uncontaminated place of God.

Night comes early in December in Montecito. By five o'clock, I turned off the computer and went back into the cottage for a quick nap before meeting Andrea and Robert Graves for the Christmas cantata.

The telephone roused me from a deep and tranquil siesta. It was Robert asking me to meet them at Pierre Lafond's in Montecito Village. They wanted to pick up some desserts and pastries for the children's reception after the musical program.

I dressed quickly and headed down winding San Ysidro Lane into the tiny village. Robert and Andrea were loaded down with enough sugar plums and New York cheesecakes to feed several shelters.

As I waited for them, I saw a basket full of white candles in old-fashioned brass holders. A card on a gold string attached to the candlesticks said: These candles are guaranteed to give off pure white light—Benedictine Order.

"Robert, how many singers will there be in the cantata tonight?"

"I know exactly how many. Twelve boys and twelve girls will sing tonight," he said.

I counted the candles and holders twice. Each time I got the same number: twenty-four candles and twenty-four holders. Was this a coincidence or a sign to follow my hunch?

On the way to the church, Andrea explained that the children singing tonight were from an orphanage, and Robert was one of its board members. Robert shared that he had been raised in such a refuge and promised himself that he would one day support orphaned children.

When we arrived at the church, a hysterical choir leader ran up to Robert in a panic. "Oh, Mr. Graves, we are ready for the concert, but the electric lights that the boys and girls were going to hold never arrived. What are we going to do?"

I stepped forward, holding out my box.

"Will these do?" I asked.

When the distraught woman saw what I had in the box, she clasped her hands to her cheeks and exclaimed, "Praise the Lord. You've brought candles. How did you know?" she asked.

She hugged me with one arm and grabbed the candles and holders with the other hand and took off for the choir loft in the rear of the church.

Robert and Andrea and I went into the church and sat near the back. We were a few minutes early, so I got to see the children light their candles. But I also got to witness something else. In preparation for the concert, the now-content choir director was at the piano. With one hand directing, she hit a note for them to sing. They were vocalizing.

"Do, re, mi, fa, so, la, ti, do." "Do, re, mi, fa, so, la, ti, do," and on and on. White candles ablaze, the children practiced their musical scales. Heaven had conspired with the littlest angels to bring the true meaning of Christmas to us that night.

The concert of twenty-four earthly cherubs went off without a hitch or a sour note. No sound is more touching than a choir of children singing their Christmas carols with all the gusto their lungs can manage. The innocence and the purity of these young boys and girls reminded me of when I sang in the All-City Christmas Cantata in Birmingham as a boy of ten. The difference between these youngsters and me as a kid was the carefree manner in which they sang. I remembered too well how separated my insides were from what I showed to the outside world. This *Silent Night, Holy Night* pageant was healing and comforting to the little boy inside me.

We were little more than a couple of miles from the San Ysidro Ranch, so I opted to leave the reception early and walk back. The weather was nippy and crisp, but I had my little-kid carolers singing in my head to keep me company.

On the edge of the ranch, I took a long walk into an elevated wooded area with a jogging path, holding a flashlight furnished by the Ranch. I saw deer and possum, flying squirrels, and ducks from the nearby pond. The fragrances of foliage and flowers reminded me of smells from my childhood.

What have I learned about myself and love? When I am open and receptive to whom and what God puts in my life, the nature of love is effortless. If I continue to clear away what separates me from love, love finds me. I am so peaceful and euphoric in the presence of love's essence. I am so full of gratitude tonight. Love is all around me if I can open myself to it.

In Buddhism, according to Thich Nhat Hanh, a Vietnamese Zen Buddhist monk who was nominated by Martin Luther King for the Nobel Peace Prize, there are four elements of true love. He describes them in his book *True Love*. The first is loving-kindness or benevolence; the second is compassion. Compassion is not only the desire to ease the pain of another person, but the ability to do it. The third element of true love is joy. Hanh says that without joy there can be no true love. And the fourth is freedom. When you love, you bring freedom to the person you love.

When I was a little boy, I yearned for someone to love me who knew me. When I was a little boy, I wanted someone who knew me to connect with me. And when I was a little boy, I wanted someone who connected with me to show me, not tell me about, love.

I did not feel loved by my family, nor was I able to love them. Later I learned that they did not have love to give. Nor did I. The church's version of God's love did not click with me, either. Too many strings were attached to the love of God as the church laid it out.

I survived on self-righteous indignation in my down-the-rabbit-hole asylum. Inside myself, I talked to an invisible friend and listened to the music in my head. Going to school and trying to get along with family and friends were like personal appearances by "the entertainer" and "the pleaser." They were my false selves.

Love came to me through insanity in a no-exit play I wrote myself into. Booze was an elixir and comfort that emboldened me to rip and tear at everything and everybody when my craziness got too much for me to tolerate. I found a lot of wild and nutty people who would drive drunk with me with no headlights on and who lived life with no roadmap and no God.

Love came to me one dark and dreary night when, going the wrong way on a one-way street, the cops pulled me over and took me to jail. Sitting in that cell, I knew that I would either die or stop drinking and learn how to live booze-free—with honesty and integrity. The minute I surrendered and admitted that I was in a sanitarium with no locks and a prison with no guards, God walked into my life, albeit abiding with me through prayer and meditation. I found that God loved me and connected with me. He really, really did love me and care for me. This was an open door to freedom to love me and to love someone else.

When I was a teenager, my minister's wife, Margaret Bowles, loved me as God would one day love me, but I could not accept her pure love. I was not ready to love and be loved.

Some cockamamie twisted notion about lover relationships settled into my subconscious with a hard-rock thud and grew like ragweed. The screwy flash-bulb light that penetrated my pitch-black rat hole told me that there were too many rotten gut-line fish hooks in romantic love. The kind of love I craved was to be held, coddled, and cuddled, without having to prove myself loveable—or to be who they needed for me to be—in order to receive their love.

As I aged, pulp fiction and B movies took away the innocence of intuitively connecting with someone I just "knew" I was meant to meet and love. Fatuous haute couture models and studly cel-luloid boys so distorted what any of us could expect; thank God I found booze instead of trying to use these apparitions of illusions as roles for me to cast myself into.

As I got older, my cad of an ego goaded me to investigate the family fortunes of a couple of girlfriends to see if there was enough lucre to put me in the lap of luxury. I needed to validate my false social pretenses. My best-laid plan backfired. On a whim and in less than six weeks from the day we met, I married a dead-broke heiress who needed someone to support her. This was the time of my life when I was either drinking alcoholically nightly or nursing a hangover. It was time for me to grow up and take responsibility for a wife. So what did I do to face the music like a man? I ran away.

When I was getting sober and recovering from "poor-little-ole-me-itis," my sponsor Bob told me to do for someone else what I would have liked for someone to have done for me. "Albert, if no one ever took you by the hand and showed you the ropes of life, get over it by taking someone else by the hand and helping him find his place in the sun—the life God has for him if he can stop drinking and drugging." Enter Scott.

When I met Scott he was waiting tables, and he did not look anything like the one I would take by the hand and help learn life's lessons. He was snarly and beefed-up with a Fu Manchu moustache. But the still, small voice said, "That's him." And I reflected back to the predictions by psychics Lena from Brazil and Bill Corrado in Los Angeles: *When you are around 60 years old, you will meet someone who has been your son in a former life; help him.* I befriended Scott—brought him into recovery—appointed myself as his sponsor—and all these years later, he and I are business partners. He travels the world to learn from the people, places, and things he meets along the way.

Scott has been the true joy of my life. What has caused our friendship to thrive is that we tell each other exactly how we feel, and we never lie about anything. We disagree but we stay with a problem until it is resolved. Scott is his own person, and so am I. Love after sobriety has been different than stabs at giving and receiving love when I was a drunk.

My client relationships thrive because they are born out of honesty. I am who my clients need for me to be. They use me as a mirror to see themselves. I had no idea that I would not only heal but would fall into the essence of twenty-four-carat-gold love while leading clients to find their authentic selves. That is the miracle of what I do. My clients are my loves, and in spite of the rough row I make them hoe, I thrive when I am working. Second only to God, work is my love and my life.

I lay still in an open field and stretched out my arms.

I wanted to stay here just as long as my soul needed to be under the midnight starry wintry sky in my favorite part of the world—Montecito, California. I asked my guru if I could move to the grounds of the Sarada Convent, build a house, and live there until I die. He said, "Stay where you are." I am still in Sedona.

I had come to realize that there were two worlds—the world of illusion and the world of reality. One was filled with fear and false creations of a divided self as ruled by the ego, and the other promised that all there is is love. I am now at the good part of the play, and I love it.

Another bellwether of love for my soul growth was Mrs. Arthur Hornblow, Jr., whom I knew as Leonora but café society called "Bubbles." The moment she walked into my life, I knew that I was the cosmic *consigliere,* but she was in charge of everything else. Leonora was tough, and she could be profane. When someone hurt me or caused me to withdraw because of their harsh words or actions, she was all over the detractor's case. She would say things like "You are the best person who ever lived on this planet, and I know because I know most anybody who is worth knowing and you are tops. Get them out of your life. Rescind the association by chanting, 'Evil spirit, go back to your keeper.'"

When Leonora disapproved of something I told her I intend-ed to do, she would say to me, "Darling, that's the dumbest thing I've ever heard. If you do such an idiotic thing, never call me again." But she loved me by her actions, and when my soul was sore she had the balm.

Mrs. Hornblow was the leading lady God chose to coddle me and cuddle me—to spoil me rotten—and to see the best in me. If I know what love is, she gave me the vocabulary.

The latest true friends—the family I always wanted—to come into my life with unconditional love were the Bells—David and Gail and their children, Ashley and Andrew. David knows how to make me laugh, and he loves me when I cannot love myself. Gail is a brilliant actress, very beautiful, but more important, she is very giving and loving. When she calls me up, she always wants to know, "What can I do for you?"

The children stir my envy when I realize how much more special they are than I have ever been. Ashley has the finest operatic soprano voice I have ever heard outside the Met and La Scala. When she was very young, I predicted she would go to Yale. At the time she was somewhat leery of me and my prognostications. She travels the world and loves Italians and Spaniards and Germans and anybody else at all ports of call. Her love is carried with vibrato and genius resonance. I see love in her face.

Andrew was born intuitive—he knows things other people don't know, as I did when I was a kid. It is so refreshing to have a prodigy of love teach me, even though he calls me his teacher. This tall, rugged, and handsome basketball and tennis star changes the world with love every day as he walks through crowds like the Pied Piper with one mission: to make those he meets better people. If I am alive when he finishes college, I want him on my Sedona Intensive team.

The Bells had brought love of family back into my life. The big difference between them and my family was the honesty with which we communed. We laugh silly at everything. Andrew and I help one another stay clearer when we watch tennis. We definitely have our favorites, and when someone we don't like wins, we can act like two-year-olds. Ashley vocalizes all day long, which raises the vibration in the house and in our hearts. The love I feel toward them and from them must be what God intended, because He laughs out loud with us.

From childhood, I learned that nobody loved me—that something was wrong with me—from the fractured intelligence of my parents and teachers, who were products of their parents and teachers, rather than opening the door to remembering on my own. Angels awaited my willingness to let go of the world of illusion and embrace the light of the world God created. Awareness of the real world was not enough to let me act in accordance with divine principle. I had to first become aware of the rules of return to God's world and let go of false doctrines, mores, and customs of the ego world.

Love has its requirements. If you hurt someone, quickly amend it by humble admission. Glamour girls may be appeased by flowers and oversized bling, but true love springs from the way we nurture rather than needle one another. If you care for someone in the name of love, show it by how you treat her, rather than with materialism. I am astounded by the number of people who measure love by what money can buy.

If you love someone, write him a love letter. Start by making amends for anything stupid or thoughtless you have done, to clear the air. Love blossoms with kind and considerate amendments to the way a relationship has sputtered.

After I cleared away all the hurt and pain and guilt I had held about my parents, I wrote them love letters loaded with forgiveness.

Dear Mother:

You know that I have struggled with my feelings about you and me since I was a youngster. I thought you were tough and I always wanted you to love me, and I don't think that you ever have. Throughout my childhood, more than anything, I wanted you to take joy in who I was and what I accomplished. I never felt that you did, until my perceptions of what happened changed.

Mother, please forgive me for being angry with you because you didn't show up when I won the spelling bee, or read a poem in the citywide contest, or was in a play, or made the National Honor Society. Someone pointed out to me that you were a single mother working five-and-a-half days a week to support six children. You were doing what you had to do. I saw you as a martyr when I should have seen you as a caring mother.

I accused you of being ashamed of me, when in truth I did not accept myself. Blaming you for my club feet and being short in stature has nearly destroyed me. When I labeled you self-righteous, I was describing my own worst defect of character. I was the drunk, not you. You co-signed loans and I never paid them, because I was trying to get back at you. Now I know that the circumstance God created for me were my opportunity to succeed with God's continuing guidance. But I left God and you in my wake.

I ask you to forgive me for how I harmed you. My amends will be to treat my life as God's business, not mine. When I see a chance to do for someone else I will, in your name.

I have a picture of you on my desk. When I look at it I whisper, "I love you, Mom."

Please forgive me,

Albert

I wrote my father a love letter as well. His was easier, because he and I are so alike. Writing him was similar to the letter I wrote myself.

Dear Dad:

It has been so much easier to blame you for all the bad that happened to me rather than to look at me. When I look at you, I see myself. I didn't have to walk away from six children to identify with you; I never had the courage to be unselfish enough to have a relationship where I could have children.

I want you to know that I love you. The humor I have comes from your gene pool; the ability to get along with anyone, rich or poor, was a quality you passed along to me as well. No one told a better story than you did, nor was better able to be a friend to someone—going to any lengths to make their life better. The greatest gift you passed along to me was laughter. As poor as we were growing up—even though you were an absentee parent—you could always see the slightest hint that dark clouds were about to open up to a sky full of possibilities.

But most of all I love you because loving you lets me love me. The one thing that I have always wanted (without knowing it) is self-love. There is nothing better than writing my soul twin to say through it all, "I love my Dad."

I love you,

Albert

Rain drizzled in my face as I lay alone in the grass. Falling stars streaked through the sky. Baby rabbits came to my chest and nibbled on carrots that were in my shirt pocket. I got up and ambled down the grassy hills and onto the converging paths that led to my cottage. The phone rang as I walked through the door.

"Hello, this is Albert."

"Albert, this is Victor. I'm just having hot coffee and fresh French bread. Does it make you jealous?" We both chuckled, because I always dashed for coffee and hot baguettes when we were in Paris. "I have two weeks off beginning Sunday. The whole command will be away on an operation that doesn't include me," he stated, with more to come. I could sense it.

"Well, I can't come back to France. I have no more francs," I said.

"I want to come to Sedona and work through some of the difficulties I've been having. Remember the issues we talked about
in Sedona and here in France?" he said.

"If you think a killer baby SEAL can survive a Sedona Intensive, come ahead. But I warn you, you may not like what you
find," I added to elicit a response.

Victor said that he would take his chances that a Sedona Intensive was no more grueling than SEAL training. I told him that
I would arrange for his accommodations at a local resort.

The Sedona Intensive would be new and challenging. Working with a soul whom I had known many lifetimes would offer
insights into my life, as well, and would reveal why Victor and I
had come back together at this time.

I sat at my desk in the cottage and made a rough outline of
how I would proceed with the intensive and what other therapists
I would use. There would be meditation hikes, intense sessions
with a psychologist and life history meetings with me, and other
pampering therapies like hot lava-rock massages, voice therapy
and Network Chiropractic adjustments. Everything seemed to
come together.

As I made a schedule for the young navy SEAL, I doodled
Brother Victor over and over again.

It would be intriguing to see what Victor and I would do to
change each other's lives. I knew that his discoveries will be about
me, also.

I got into bed with my headphones and fell sleep reciting 1
Corinthians 13 while listening to Deva Premal.

Though I speak with the tongues of men and of angels, and have not love, I am become as sounding brass, or a tinkling cymbal.

And though I have the gift of prophecy, and understand all mysteries, and all knowledge; and though I have all faith, so that I could remove mountains, and have not love, I am nothing.

And though I bestow all my goods to feed the poor, and though I give my body to be burned, and have not love, it profiteth me nothing.

Love suffereth long, and is kind; love envieth not; love vaunteth not itself, is not puffed up,

Doth not behave itself unseemly, seeketh not her own, is not easily provoked, thinketh no evil;

Rejoiceth not in iniquity, but rejoiceth in the truth;

Beareth all things, believeth all things, hopeth all things, endureth all things.

Love never faileth: but whether there be prophecies, they shall fail; whether there be tongues, they shall cease; whether there be knowledge, it shall vanish away.

For we know in part, and we prophesy in part.

But when that which is perfect is come, then that which is in part shall be done away.

When I was a child, I spake as a child, I understood as a child, I thought as a child: but when I became a man, I put away childish things.

For now we see through a glass, darkly; but then face to face: now I know in part; but then shall I know even as also I am known.

And now abideth faith, hope, and love, these three; but the greatest of these is love.

Chapter 11

Swami and the End of the Journey

I relaxed at the San Ysidro Ranch for another day. My recovery sponsor's wife Gloria arrived mid-afternoon. Gloria and I have known one another since I got sober, and she was the first speaker I heard when I entered recovery. I will never forget that night when she said from the podium, "My name is Gloria and I'm an alcoholic. Tonight I feel clean inside, because I've gotten rid of all secrets and shame from my years of drinking and running with outlaws. If anybody in this meeting is looking for an easier, softer way, this is the best deal in town. This is the only way that worked for me."

Gloria and I decided to have an early supper alone. I wanted to tell her what had happened to me. She was the one person I could say anything to and she would remain open-minded.

"Gloria, I want to tell you all that I have found out about myself through meditation and a High Self consciousness," I said.

Through the long story about Paul and the lessons, she didn't say a word. She listened, and I intuited that she believed me.

"I have lived thousands of lives, famous and infamous—both as a man and as a woman—some as a good little boy or girl, and a lot where I was a bad apple. I chose my parents and siblings because they provided the proper DNA, family dysfunctions, and also positive qualities that would best help me fulfill my destiny.

"I am not who you think I am, and neither are you. I chose alcoholism to help me tear down who I am not; I failed at life in order to rebuild from the rack and ruin as who I am. I have endured major struggles with my sexuality, because I needed to discover that I am soulfully both male and female. When I conquer the desire body, the soul man emerges. The desire body is how my ego has kept me trapped in an identity that was not mine.

"We have told one another since we met twenty-five years ago that we love the good life. You said that we both like to sponsor newcomers trying to get sober. It is amazing how often my ego has swooped in to give me something that I think I want only to grow tired and depressed from the very thing I longed for. And it is just as painful to face what God takes away from me," I said.

Gloria's faith and trust in God were tested harshly when her oldest child, Bobby, sober for eight years after living on the streets, abusing heroin, and engaging in prostitution, died of AIDS in 1990. His passing was not a matter of slipping quietly through the veil into what we call death. It took weeks and weeks for Bobby to die. He suffered horribly. Gloria agonized. His sister Lisa sang and laughed with her brother until the end. They all cried and asked, "Why Bobby?"

After dinner, we drove the serpentine East Valley Road to the Sarada Convent on Ladera Lane. Our first stop was the bookstore. I bought a copy of Eknath Easwaran's *The End of Sorrow*, a commentary on the *Bhagavad Gita*, and handed it to Gloria.

"Just to make sure that there's no more unfinished business about Bobby, read this. You'll be freer than you've been since the day you got sober," I said.

"What is it about?"

"It is the story of how human beings, like Don Quixote, fight windmills, but our difficulties—the wars we wage—are of our own making. The book helps you to meditate and make peace within you. Read it, Gloria."

She and I strolled to the temple a few yards away and, after removing our shoes, walked in and sat down and began to meditate.

After half an hour, Gloria and I walked out together and took a side path to oleander and cymbidium flower beds. We sat on the ground and looked out at the starry skies toward the Pacific Ocean. A full moon lit up the night.

"I feel clean inside. Remember when you said how clean you felt the first time I heard you speak, Gloria? God is finally helping me let go of the bondage of self and others. I see with new eyes," I said quietly.

"I feel quiet peace and tranquility. I came today with sadness and regret. The temple has a special energy. Were angels present in the temple, Albert?"

"Angels are everywhere, Gloria. You and I are not who we think we are. We are fallen angels rediscovering the power of God within ourselves."

"Bobby is an angel, I just know it. Angels wrapped their wings around my son and took him to Paradise." Gloria's voice cracked with emotion as she spoke.

"Come over here under this tree. Let's meditate together. I am going to do something with you that I've never done. We are going to attempt to get Paul to speak through me about Bobby," I said to Gloria as we sat beneath a spreading oak.

Within minutes we both were in a relaxed state. Through me Paul spoke aloud to Gloria:

You came here today, Gloria, looking for a sign.

"I am looking for a sign for what?" Gloria asked.

You want a sign that Bobby's soul is alive.

Crickets started evening anthems. Foghorns blared from distant boats. In the moment, still minds and electric telepathy converged somewhere between Heaven and the mountaintop.

When you think thoughts that make you feel love, angels are in the field. As you clear away all blocks and barriers to your true identity, you activate angelic memory and draw the energies to you, from among yourselves, and from Paradise.

Walk in the light. Become one from within, where God is. Never start the journey back without a brother. Know that love is all there is, and you will identify with the angel you are.

Angels who restore and reclaim original progeny remain on Earth to rebuild the God connection.

Earth can be as Heaven when the souls of the angelic realm begin to grow in number.

When a pilgrim returns home through death, sickness, accident, or old age, his soul goes through a period of adjustment. There are no accidents. Every minute detail of a life is preordained.

Souls who come back must go through reform school and a vibration detoxification. As you must return with a brother or sister, spirit angels are in service to you and to others. When someone dies and returns to Heaven, he cannot communicate with you during his period of quarantine.

Do you have any questions?

Gloria still wanted to know if Bobby was alive in the afterlife and if he was happy.

Today in the Sarada bookstore, Albert gave you an angel as a sign.

There was silence but for the sound of wind. Gloria swallowed and began to breathe rapidly, for her own intuition would not allow her to conceal her joy.

Gloria, someone wants to speak to you.

"I love you, Mom," a faint, soft voice spoke.

"I love you, Bobby."

The next morning I took a morning walk after breakfast with Swami in the high hills on Bella Vista.

"Swami, I know who I am. I know I'm not who everybody thinks I am. I'm not even who I thought I was. I'm a precious child of God who must bring my brother with me on my journey back to my authentic self," I spoke hurriedly.

"Ramapriya, I remember once when you came to me and said, 'Who am I?' To what do you owe this new awareness?" he asked.

I stopped on the road for a second.

"I got still enough to hear God when He spoke to me. Ramapriya became teachable enough to let go of the will of the ego and be who he has always been," I added.

"Is your mind calm enough to tell me the true meaning of lesson five, which says that men and women are the same?" he asked.

"None of us is really a man or a woman, but we are both. We must embrace the androgyny of consciousness to be able to discover who we are. A child is born to correct lost soul conditions from prior lives that have perpetuated his false self. When we die, based upon what we have cleared and cleaned up of past transgressions, we can return to the perfect place where God lives."

"You seemed to have remembered a lot on your journey to clear away the wreckage of present and past lives. But what about the rest of lesson five: you're not who you think you are?" Swami continued.

"No one has the key to who we are; rather our true self is revealed within us. The reason we cannot know true self is because our egotistical false self has played a game that has kept us from who we are. Mother sees us as her child and trains us in her ways and with her impressions of who we are and what we need to do with our lives. A lover sees us as what he needs us to be to fit his needs, his expectations. The church needs for us to be the sinner so its dogma can save us.

"The ego-created world of material illusion is created outside man. The illusionary world is an enemy to the angel that he is," I answered.

"You are speaking of the Atman, Ramapriya. And lesson six?" he asked.

"The lesson, forgiveness is the path to clearing, tells us that we must make amends to ourselves and others or we will not be able to let go of the wreckage of the past. Hurting oneself is as destructive as harming somebody else. It is the lesson that frees us from all the dirt, guilt, and shame of past misdeeds. Through forgiveness we cut the umbilical cord to people, places, and things that are connected to the ledger of our miscreant self. Seek forgiveness, and that person or situation will never come back into your life," I said.

"Continue with seven and eight. I need to hear while you are so clear," Swami cajoled me with his humor.

"Lesson seven says that you are your brother's keeper. This one stumped me for a while, because I thought that brother's keeper was archaic Old Testament truth that was outmoded with the birth, life, death, and resurrection of Christ consciousness," I said.

"Your problem, Ramapriya, is that you confuse God's truth with man's heresy. Now give me the clear answer, please," he requested.

I never feel shamed by Swami, only amended to better understanding.

"We are all interconnected and interrelated. Each of us returns to Earth one by one, but we are able to find our way home in twos or more. The ancient teachings caution us to share what we receive—to love thy brother as thyself—never to receive for the self alone. The road home requires that we come back with our brother, who represents the dark side of ourselves. We project our shadow selves onto our enemies, who teach us more than our friends. Love and embrace your shadow, recognize it as the dark part of God—the Great Deceiver—and convert it with love, and you will be as who you really are.

"Lesson eight says that love is the Great Redeemer, God's glue that holds His fallen angels together as they help one another—with no payoff and no motive but to let the God within us love his fellowman," I said.

Squirrels scampered and dogs barked, and we continued to walk together in silence. The teacher said nothing, and the student began to learn that not all correct responses would be rewarded with praise.

Swami spoke again.

"I have changed my mind about where you should live and where you should work. If it is still your pleasure, you may come here to Montecito and live at the monastery. You will be of great assistance to our caretaker, Anadi."

I sat down in the middle of the road and cupped my face. Then I jumped up and hopped around like the little kid I had just rescued from his rat hole of shame.

"No. No. No. No, Swami. Don't you see? I don't need to hide out at the monastery here in Montecito. I know what I am supposed to do. I know my purpose. God is working through me. When the client comes to me, he comes as me. When the client heals, I heal. With your blessing, I will continue to see God in all my clients. God touches me every single day, even when I do not know He is reaching out to me. But as you said, 'see God in others long enough and God will reach out and touch you.' Well, He has and He does, through the clients who counsel with me," I proffered.

Swami smiled and we continued to walk.

"Well, since you won't make me tea and listen to my lectures in the temple or comfort the devotees when they come, perhaps it is best for you to remain in Sedona as long as it is God's will. You once said to me that God does not care where you work and where you live; He cares how you work and how you live," Swami said.

We walked a few steps and my teacher continued. "For now, Ramapriya, I think I want to take that turn there," Swami said, pointing to a right-turn dirt-road intersection.

"God wants to show you something on a road you have never traveled. Are you willing?"

He was walking faster, and I hastened to catch up, chattering excitedly.

"Swami," I cried out as I picked up pace, "I have one last question. Paul says that all of us are trying to go home. He talks about Heaven. Just where is Heaven?"

He stopped and turned to me with a big grin on his face.

"All this time you are gathering lessons that will take you and others to Heaven and you don't know where you are going?" Swami laughed loudly and his merriment caused tears of joy to flood his face.

"Aha ha, ha ha, Ramapriya, you are so amusing and amazing. The kingdom of Heaven is quite near to you."

He took his long brown finger and tapped it on my chest. "The kingdom of Heaven is within," he said calmly.

For a moment or two neither of us moved. Our eyes involuntarily closed, and we began to breathe in and breathe out. Silent and still on the dusty road, my teacher led me through Heaven's gate. I was home. The search for Paradise was over. Swami Swahananda again broke into a brisk pace. I stood where I was. As I came back to the present, I realized that once again the teacher was far ahead of the student.

I raced after Swami, shouting.

"Swami, the most incredible thing happened last evening. My friend Gloria spoke with her son Bobby, who is an angel in Heaven, and you wouldn't believe…"

And the wise man and the fool trudged the winding back roads of God's panorama, speaking of cabbages and kings and hills that God built for man to climb. A large band of angels walked with these pilgrims to keep them company in the beautiful verdant mountains of Montecito.

Book II

Retrieving in Sedona:
The Sedona Intensive

Introduction

Sedona, located 100 miles north of Phoenix off I-17, is known as Red Rock Country because she is nestled in a valley of craggy reddish-brown sandstone formations millions of years old. If you look closely, hundreds of etched figures appear to stand guard over this rustic hamlet.

At sunset the rock colors darken and appear gothic and majestic. Named for the daughter of an early pioneer, the city boasts more than ten vortexes. Spiritual wisdom contends that a vortex, a whirling, circular mass of energy, is either electric, magnetic, or electromagnetic—masculine, feminine, or androgynous—and carries a vibration that has healing properties.

When the weary traveler climbs the highly charged rocks, he feels something enchanting and magical. Many claim to have been healed or cleared of emotional despair. Sedona's mystical beauty has dubbed her the Egypt of America. Her transcendent alchemy makes the spiritually aware refer to her as "the bridge across forever."

Locals know that Sedona will beckon you. She will put you under her hypnotic spell. If your energy is not aligned with hers, Sedona will drive you out as quickly as she drew you in.

My clients are drawn here to clear away the wreckage of their pasts that keep them from becoming who God created them to be. Each experiences the Sedona Intensive in his own special way. Each confesses that he arrives as a prodigal in the death-grip of his ego and leaves as a happy, joyous, and free precious child of God.

Chapter 1

Discover You

"How do I deal with having been sexually molested by my father?" Deborah asked with those brown saucer eyes pleading for help for the ten-year-old inner child she was trying to rescue from the rat holes of shame. I had been recommended to her by a woman from Santa Fe, New Mexico, who was famous for putting students and teachers together.

Deborah called and booked an initial session on the telephone. An Intensive followed two weeks later. Clients find the Intensive by recommendation only. We never advertise. When someone inquires about the program, we send out a brochure in the colors of the red rocks.

Our program began in 1982. One by one they found us: addicts and alcoholics who were facing insanity or a wet brain, as well as men and women who needed help adjusting to being fired from a job, facing a divorce that came out of nowhere, or grieving the death of a spouse or other family member. They were all desperate to find out who they were.

I am amazed at what compassion and understanding do for suffering souls. Throughout my trials and tragedies growing up, the one thing I never lost was my ability to get people to tell me their deepest, darkest secrets—no matter how sordid or sick they were.

Our unique therapy model was built on the solid rock of getting at the truth of who did what to whom, no matter how much pain the client had to endure. Clearing digs up taproots of denial and cleans up all the toxins buried in family secrets. "Hear no evil, see no evil, speak no evil" are the same three monkeys that keep us suffering in silence.

Harriet Hilburn of Phoenix, Arizona—CEO of a large art studio who has sent many employees as well as herself through our program—advises those who need our program, "Go everywhere else first before coming to Albert. He will get in your face—nose to nose and toes to toes—grab your ego by the throat, and dare it not to let go."

Deborah's "Once upon a time…" opened with her tale of sexual addiction and how it began. She got to that part of her story by simply following the syllabus of recovery like all the clients do:

>   Homework, Part One:
>   Write me about your family.
>   Talk to me about who God is to you.
>   Tell me about your sexual history.

Deborah discovered in long-haul therapy with a super psychologist, through flashbacks and nightmares, that her father had not only abused her sexually but also had allowed his good-old-boys' club members to do the same. Listening to her painful and agonizing recount was hard to stomach.

She had graduated with honors from a first-rate college and edited the law review in law school. And while she had taken her father to court and settled for big bucks before the case ever came to trial, she had never done any emotional closure on the sexual abuse.

Enter Albert and his support team of therapists.

After I heard everything that I could, plumbed all shameful sinkholes, and shone a light into every secret hiding place in the theaters of Deborah's mind to make sure we had seen everything significant, together we evaluated what had happened to her. I always let the client take all the time they need to get the story in plain sight. Editing or leading the storyteller can hamper the trust you need to establish with the damaged, distrusting child within them.

The adult will always call upon the ego to minimize the damage to her perception of herself. To get around the unconscious red herring of the adult, open up dialogue with her shame-based child, and you will get at the truth of what's wrong and when it started. The child will never lie. The adult always will. The adult will do anything to stonewall and cover up. Use the love of God and be honest with the child within the adult, and the child will respond to truth and trust you to hear his or her story of shame. She needs for someone to believe her.

"What has all this family history shown you, Deborah?" I asked.

"That my mother probably knew about the sexual abuse and did nothing," she answered.

"Why did she do nothing? Was she a bad mother? Do you think she was evil?" I asked.

"She didn't know how. The child within her who had never gotten to speak to anyone about her fears was afraid of my father," she whispered, blinking back tears and wiping them with an unsteady hand.

"Is it safe to say that your mother was unable to give you something she didn't have: the emotional and psychological stability to confront your father?" I asked.

"Yes."

"Could the same thing be said about your father? If your mother has never been able to free the terrified child within herself, could your father have a hurt and abused child acting out of his own shame? Could your father have been sexually abused when he was a young boy?"

Deborah had been through years of therapy, meditation weekends, and bodywork and had kept a journal from early days of working with a therapist. In a moment of clarity at the end of day three of our program, she realized that she could not go on with her anger and rage and blame of her father. In a split second of supreme shift from who she thought she was to who God created her to be, Deborah found a profound love for her father that had eluded her for forty-three years.

Deborah was able to accept that her father's inability to be close and intimate with her and her sister and their mother was the result of his not having been nurtured and loved as a boy. She began to relate to him and his suffering and to have empathy for his struggles.

She never denied how brutal her father's behavior had been, but she needed to forgive herself and him. If she didn't, the inability to forgive her father would keep her playing the blame game, and the unfinished business would keep her sick

As I listened to her story, my mind went back to other clients who had dealt with sexual abuse issues. A man, whom I'll call Daniel, from a tiny town in Arkansas, was a handsome and successful trial lawyer. Athletic and charismatic, Daniel could lead a jury to his point of view with sheer mastery. He had the world on a string, pulling in big fees and dating the most beautiful women in town. He had everything, including a compulsion to expose himself to young children, masturbating while they watched. After he had been arrested, part of his plea agreement was that he had to get professional help. He came for an Intensive.

Together I and my therapists discovered that Daniel had low self-esteem and unresolved secrets around his sexuality—he had been fondled as a child by a minister. He had also engaged in a lot of anonymous sexual encounters with both men and women while in college. Daniel's mother had been a dominant single parent with no boundaries, and she had never bonded in a loving, caring way with her son. He cleared by facing secrets, seeing himself and others as doing the best they could with what they had—but only after raging at his perpetrators and then forgiving himself and them—and facing the shame that had imprisoned him from infancy. He stopped trying to be the all-American man with all the answers; rather he exposed all the shame, dirt, and guilt that had been destroying his life. Prescription: regular Sex and Love Addicts Anonymous meetings and ongoing group therapy have kept Daniel free from acting out of his sexual disease for over three years.

We further discovered the two reasons why he had never gotten help. First, he had never been arrested and humiliated; and second, he had never taken a thorough and honest inventory of his life. Daniel admitted that he was powerless over his addiction and that his life had become unmanageable. Square one was surrender. To maintain abstinence for the rest of his life one step at a time, he had to go to meetings, write in his journal, and pray daily to a God of his own understanding.

A wise old woman from New York City with over forty years of sobriety once told me, "A life uninventoried is a life not worth living."

"Moments and windstorms," said Elisabeth Kübler-Ross, M.D., author of *On Death and Dying*, "are what we remember when we are dying." Houses and cars and fancy clothes, she felt, pale in comparison with what really counts in life, like the birth of a baby or the graduation from college of a son or daughter. These life events comprise the golden memories that nurture and sustain us.

When I am asked how our brand of therapy works, I shrug and admit that I don't know. "If it works, it's right." If asked about what makes us different from other therapies, I don't compare ours with other programs; instead, I tell the questioner that our method is to peel back the layers of a client's childhood and tap into his cellular memory of feelings of anger and rage. Then he must see the family for who they really are, cop an honest plea about his part in the melodrama, and then get on with his life. Acceptance that everybody is doing the best they can with what they have is a major step toward being released from shackles of the past. But the real distinction of our program is that God is at the heart of the process.

"I look at all of you as fallen angels who are trying to become who God created you to be." When I was getting sober in Long Beach, California, a toothless and unwashed longshoreman said in a meeting, 'God created me to be one thing, and I was determined to be something else.' I was addressing a reunion of clients who had been through the Sedona Intensive. "All the things we do to get our own way, to come into compliance with a faulty ego, are a separation-from-God problem. The entire week I try to escort you back to who God created you to be. You look at the mess you've made, separate what's a keeper from what has to go, write letters of anger and rage, and then forgive yourself and others."

Troy was another client who had bottled up so much anger and rage that he could have erupted into violence at any moment. From Houston, Texas, Troy was a robust, determined man who had struggled with homosexuality and his mother's reaction to it. When he came to Sedona in 1994, he was in a job he didn't like and a relationship that needed honest appraisal, and his smoldering temper tantrums needed to be dealt with. Although Troy was pleasant and sociable, he had an edge that kept people at a distance from fear of what he might say or do at any given moment.

Not only did Troy's mother reject him, but she had kept him from seeing his grandmother—her mother, who had raised Troy from infancy—as she lay dying. And at her death, his mother left Troy nothing of her estate worth several million dollars.

When we got into his inventory, it was apparent that Troy's inner child was mad as hell at how he had been treated and was determined to rule Troy's adult life until the day he died. The resentful child within Troy colored how Troy growled at life and how life recoiled from his anger.

"Learn to listen and listen to learn," my first sober group sponsor hammered into me. This admonition pays off daily from my side of the work we do. The art of listening to his inner child made Troy begin to trust that what he was learning here just might work.

I have never worked with one client or met one person in a twelve-step meeting who did not exhibit inordinate fear. Fear is always fuel looking for a match. Those who mask fear usually suffer from denial. Their walls of defense will eventually crumble under the psychic pressure of debilitating addictions or physical illness in later years.

Troy's primal fear was that no one would ever love him. If his mother hated him, why would anyone else ever care about him? His inner child suffered from being unloved and unwanted, and the only way the child knew to keep the pain in check was to lash out at others before they got close enough to hurt him. Fear of rejection and fear of never knowing true love and happiness were at the core of Troy's overeating, acting out sexually, and living with a permanent chip on his shoulder.

How did he reach a place of forgiveness and release from the bondage of self and his mother? In addition to making a laundry list of character defects, whom he had harmed and how, who had harmed him and how, and assets and liabilities (Homework, Part Two), he realized that the family karmic mirrors helped him look at what was wrong with him. He had to face what he had perpetrated on others.

"You can argue until you're blue in the face, Troy, but so much of this pain started with words and deeds centuries and lifetimes ago. Your soul knew that it was time to be free of the ties that bind you to your mother's behavior," I said.

"How exactly do the wheels of karma work?" he asked.

"You must feel every feeling you ever inflicted on someone else, and be held accountable for every deed you ever did. If you were cruel, someone will come along in some lifetime and inflict cruelty on you. Kill someone someplace in time, and you will be killed in that life or a subsequent life. Abandon children and you will live a life in which you are denied the sacred right to bear or raise children. Not one deed or one feeling goes unaccounted for.

"It is important to maintain balance in past-life belief. Not everything should be reasoned through past lives. Too many people get stuck in yesterday. Some of us use past lives as a blame game. Inventory your own life and claim responsibility for the hand life dealt you. You choose your parents, and you choose the assets and liabilities that will help you remove unwanted qualities from your life. There are no accidents and no coincidences. When you have learned certain lessons, you will be freed from negative people and situations that come into your life to make you face your defects of character."

After Troy finished his Intensive, he said with tears flooding his face, "I love my mother."

I love my mother, too. After being honest with myself and seeing that she was doing the best she could with what she had left, I found love hiding in the bushes of most of my personal and professional relationships.

Family inventory is always where the journey from darkness into light, from ego-self to God-self, begins. Acceptance of the hand life deals us is the break in the dark clouds we need to recover from all addictions and unwanted conditions. No matter what clients bring to the red-rock vortices for healing, each of them must accept life on life's terms and realize that they are the only ones they can change.

The family is the karmic mirror.

When a client sinks into morbid reflection or 'poor little ole me' syndrome, I declare vociferously, "Madame (or Sir), I don't do Baby Snooks," alluding to the archetypal crybaby of the 1940s hit radio show played by "Funny Girl" Fanny Brice. Tears of release or honor of one's pain and angst are legitimate; boo-hoos from self-pity are anathema to me, and not allowed. My friend and confidante, Leonora Hornblow, now dead and sorely missed, used to be very suspect of too many tears. She felt many of us use tears as weapons, and I tend to agree with her. Because I face the truth that I am always my problem and that I am the only one I can change, I don't allow clients to drown in remorse or regrets.

From day one, all clients who want to rid themselves of the shame that binds them seem to go through a sudden shift in the emotional body. They often arrive frightened and wondering what will happen, and when they awaken the first morning, they feel different.

Until the client lets go of what keeps him doing the same thing with the same disastrous results, he will not change; his life can get no better. One dilemma the client faces is that he has no God in his life. He lives with the lying, cheating, and distrustful ego with all its false promises. To entice the ego to die and be reborn as a precious child of God, we suggest that the client repeat words like God, truth, love, beauty, peace, balance, and harmony as a mantra. The ego cannot stand the name of God!

Some clients who go through our program project their ego issues. It is not uncommon for me to read a client's journal and find that he has transferred his own character defects onto me or one of the therapists. I grin and tell him that he has a strange way of telling me about himself. When we are disturbed by another person, it is always our own stuff we need to look at.

God is within.

The light will never fail.

Locals who wallow in metaphysical superstition give all the credit for change to the powerful alchemical properties within Sedona's vortices. This may be partially true. Perhaps some special other-worldly properties within this valley of reddish-brown carvings affect our energy bodies, and we begin to experience "wow" and "aha" phenomena. Whatever the catalyst, before the week is over, all Sedona Intensive clients go through an epiphany of transcendence: They eliminate tons and lifetimes of painful, terrifying skeletons from their closets.

Powerful energy sites like Sedona, Lourdes, Maui, Stonehenge, Mount Shasta, and Machu Picchu, as well as rousing music and plays, or inspiring books, speeches, and sermons, all set the stage for spiritual revolution of mind and body, but lasting changes come from a searching and fearless moral inventory.

We found our support team in the exceptional pool of professional practitioners who have been drawn to live and work in this mystical paradise. Each client sees at least one certified psychologist. Specialized therapists counsel the client with marriage and family dysfunction and offer great healing insights into sex and love addictions.

Curious clients ask, "Why all the other therapists?" I answer, "Some guests are sicker than others." We laugh our way through to the next step and the next level of looking at what went wrong, and when.

When I was getting sober, I was all business. I carried the weight of recovery on my face. A small group of recovering alcoholic men and I had a ritual of going fishing from my recovery sponsor's boat every Saturday morning and going to a recovery meeting that afternoon. After a day on the brine and while we ate an early supper at sponsor Fil's house, we left the lines of our anchored poles in the water hoping a fish would bite our hooks. One day I went to check the lines and screamed, "I caught some big and exotic fish. I caught the biggest fish in the ocean!" All the guys came running and began to snicker, one at a time. It dawned on me that they had put the fish on my line so that I would think I had caught a whopper. I started laughing until I cried. Once again, I was able to laugh at myself rather than be so serious.

Laugh tracks lie all over the work we do. I believe in the power and magic of not taking yourself too seriously.

I am twelve-step, experience, strength and hope-oriented, and I ask all the loaded, squirmy, creepy-crawly leading questions like: "Why have you never looked at your gay side (straight side for homosexuals)?" "Did you know untreated anger can get you the same results as the irate postal worker who walks into his workplace and kills a dozen innocent people?" "Why do you keep getting into sick bondage/hostage-like relationships? Haven't you had enough?" (To a woman): "Did it ever dawn on you that the reason you don't like men is that you have never gotten in touch with the man who lives within you?"

All who go through our program know that I use an astrology birth chart, as did renowned Swiss psychologist Dr. Carl Jung. I want to see what's going on in their lives and why they're coming to work with us at the time that they do. The birth chart also gives me a good idea of how likely they are to respond to our program. Astrology provides accurate insights into character, assets, liabilities, and windows of opportunity for momentous things to happen in one's life. I never talk astrology or do a horoscope session once the Intensive starts. Astrology is a convenient diversion to old-fashioned recovery. The client comes to recover from a hopeless state of mind and body, not to have me forecast a new lover or whether he will win the lottery or move to Xanadu.

In our program, cleaning and clearing away the wreckage of the past includes soothing massages. Looking into our childhood chambers of horrors, and getting honest enough to take action to change, not only weakens the grasp of the deceitful ego, but also takes a toll on the physical body. Attendees receive several massages by licensed body workers; work with a Wharton Performance stretch therapist; open up their throat restrictions with a vocal coach, and receive adjustments from network chiropractors.

Most people come with either top-notch or poor physical conditioning. Either they look like a bodybuilder in top-flight shape or they have never been in a gym or taken even baby steps to fitness in their entire lives. We have them go to a gymnasium no matter what condition they are in. If there are problems with eating disorders like anorexia, bulimia or obesity, we bring in a nutritionist or dietitian.

The last day, the client goes through an ancient Egyptian/ Hopi letter-burning ceremony of forgiveness, which is done on a hike led by the co-director of our program, who takes our people to the mountaintop as an inspiring ending to the magical, yet grounded, program.

In recovery circles, a popular story points out just how determined addicts are and how far they will go to get what they think they want. A mother goes into her son's room and finds him madly digging through a pile of manure.

"What are you doing?" she asks with astonishment.

"Well, Mom, I figured that with all this manure there has to be a pony here somewhere."

There is a revelation that underneath all the terrible, miserable, and scary misdeeds of their past is a silver lining breaking through the dark skies. They find great benefit from looking at everything they have done to harm themselves and others. The payoff for the painful search is when they realize who they really are.

In addition to family and sexual history, those who go through the Intensive write about harm—how he or she hurt others and how family and friends have harmed them. Who did what to whom? This part of the Intensive can be excruciating. There are often a lot of tears and a lot more anger and rage which comes up. Within the client, fear—anger turned inward—goes looking for all the horrible things everybody did to harm him. We grab their fear and wrap it in swaddling clothes and lay it and the client in the manger of deep meditation. If you can still the mind, the answers will follow. The light of God will begin to break through.

Nearing the end of the process, we have attendees write anger and rage letters. Even though the truth has dawned on the client that he is his own problem, he must still face the mean-spirited demons, wrath and fury. Like a steam whistle on a teapot, the anger and rage letters act as a release mechanism, liberating him from toxic psychic buildup. This exercise is akin to his beating a pillow with a stick or venting with Dr. Arthur Janov's primal scream.

I encourage participants to let it all hang out, to go over the top like a ham actor. Tidying and "making nice" are not appropriate in the anger and rage exercise. I warn them not to dress it up. They must force rage out of all its secret hiding places. No subject is taboo, and nothing is inappropriate except not facing every shred of rage.

They curse. They damn. They cry. They threaten. They go into the halls of shame and insanity and fight for their lives. What they are really doing is demanding that the ego reveal itself as the lying, conniving, godless, overrated overlay energy that it is. The ego has been in collusion for eons with the egos of our families, friends, and enemies to create the ultimate war of annihilation and Armageddon.

After all the blood, sweat, and years of beating himself up, the client discovers the key to all instant illumination: The war is always within; he is the only one he can change. Although we are our own problem, and each of us has an out-of-bounds ego, beneath our false personas are angels-in-waiting to help us return to God. To access our true selves, we must come to face our devils and unmask them.

Getting quiet through meditation is a required course in our program. Most clients complain that they can't stay still, that they fall asleep, and that their mind wanders. I ask them to stay the course. That we can't meditate is a measure of how frenetic our world has become. After a few days, the resistance melts, and each one begins to relax and still the mind.

The teary and hilarious stories I have heard on my journeys with these courageous seekers and searchers have served as incentives to keep me doing what I have been doing for more than twenty-five years. Those moments when the client comes out of the darkness and into the light of transformation give me goose bumps, and I say to myself, "thank God for the privilege of being a part of such a transformational time in someone's life."

I refer to myself as Charon, after the mythological boatman who ferried souls of the dead across the River Styx to eternal life. My assignment is to lovingly escort the troubled but courageous men and women who seek my counsel out of the darkness and into the light. This clearing process is a method of dying to the old way of life and being reborn as an authentic human being.

Sally Ann wrote copiously in her journal during her stay in Sedona. It was freezing outside that winter in Red Rock Country, so Sally Ann curled up in front of the fireplace in her suite and wrote and wrote and wrote. She remembered an incident from her teen years when someone had harmed her.

When she was a freshman in high school she intercepted a note being passed. The note made reference to "big blonde with the big nose," but no name was assigned to the owner of the proboscis. Sally Ann assumed that the writer was referring to her, so she stuck the note in her textbook and proceeded to carry the stigma of big-nosed blonde forever. She even looked at herself differently and longed for a nose job, when in fact her nose was fine.

"Sally Ann, did it ever occur to you that the note was not intended for you?" I was digging with search-and-rescue.

"No, I had blond hair. It was dyed, mind you, but I was blond. Who else could the note have been about?" The door of reason was ajar and I decided to stomp through.

"I hate to burst your self-centered bubble, dear heart, but perhaps another big blonde may have won by a nose over yours. Could the note have been about someone else?" I was headed for victory over selfish and self-centered thinking.

Sally Ann looked down and scrunched her small and attractive nose and said, "Gosh, I never looked at it like that!"

Sally Ann succeeded in throwing out garbage that had hurt her for twenty years. The rest of the Intensive she was fearless in looking at all her family-of-origin issues. But the trigger-point for Sally Ann was this teenage misconception that lay innocently buried. It was not physical or emotional abuse, or lying, cheating, or stealing that caused her to be less than God created her to be; rather it was clearing up a misunderstood incident in school that opened her to the sunlight of the soul.

An inventory is oftentimes necessary to stumble onto what has been causing years and years of pain and shame. An event that seems insignificant to others may be deadly to the one who has been living with it.

Sarah had been a client for more than ten years. A true Southern belle, she was raised in Sweetwater, Alabama, and had married into a prominent family. After a ten-year marriage, she and her husband decided to divorce. Vivacious, witty, and a brilliant artist, Sarah could move only so far in the art world and then her fears would paralyze her. She would change agents or her painting style; she would even move from one city to another, but she never changed what would make a big difference: her distorted perceptions of reality.

"I would love to come to Sedona, Albert, but I don't have any money," Sarah pleaded on the phone one day from Santa Fe. When I hear Southerners plead poverty, what they are generally admitting to is that they have the means to rent a beach house on the Gulf, shop until they're bankrupt, or jet off to ski or play golf ... but that investing in their mental health is a waste of money. I know; I'm a Southerner.

"Sarah, you can't afford not to come. You're nearly fifty years-old, and you aren't where you want to be in the M-and-M-and-M department: Momma, money, and men. Cash a bond or CD and book your room." I had worked with Sarah long enough to know that M for Momma stood for Virgo momma; mine was one, too. You can't put off working on a Virgo momma too long.

"I am in so much fear about spending that much money right now. I need to sell a painting in order to come do an intensive. Let's do a session this weekend and let me know what you see," Sarah said, cracking the door of willingness.

She called that weekend and at the end of the session I told her that I felt she would sell a painting and she should earmark the money for the work here if the prediction came true. On the very day that I said she would, Sarah sold a painting and called to say she was on her way to Sedona.

While she was in Sedona, we worked hard on Momma. Sarah was so like her mother it was scary. To love Momma was self-love, and to hate her was to loathe herself. She healed Momma by healing herself.

Money was about self-worth and self-esteem. Fear of losing what she had caused Sarah to hoard and hide money. She would binge-spend and then refuse to touch her checkbook and credit cards, as if they were snakes that would bite her. She turned her money, like Momma, over to God, and she got better.

Issues with men took longer. Embedded in Daddy stuff—hers left when she was eight—Sarah longed for a man not only to fix her, but to love her and to stay with her through bad times and the best of times. Together she and I did some role-playing and creative visualization to define how transferring her shadow to men was crippling her ability to see her problems as her own. If she claimed her inadequacies and used the tools we therapists had given her, she would be strong where she had always been weak. She would be able to attract men who were healthier—balanced with their internal feminine and able to have a good relationship with a woman. When our program finished, she was able to make it okay to be alone and to continue to heal herself. "In God's time, Albert, when I am healthy and God is ready, I will be open to date a man who is comfortable with himself and who identifies himself not through his partner, but through who he really is."

The most startling event of Sarah's Intensive was when she wrote forgiveness letters to her stepdaughters. Sarah had always allowed her own deficient ego to stand in the way of being a loving and caring surrogate parent to the girls, Anne and Katherine. As she read the letters, Sarah cried with joy. She felt no embarrassment at releasing the secret of why she really hadn't attended Anne's wedding and had skipped both girls' Bryn Mawr graduations. Sarah did not go because she felt less than, and invalidated by, the girls' father, Sarah's ex-husband, Barton—not because she wanted to spare the girls' feelings about having two mothers there. When Sarah told me the truth, she was released from the bondage of a dark and condemning secret.

Three years later, as her astrology birth chart indicated, Sarah met and married a sweet and loving man. He lived by the axiom that no one can make you happy but you. And that you must be happy with yourself before another person can be happy with you.

You're not who you think you are, and things are not what they seem.

"God cannot heal what He cannot see," I say to all seekers of higher truth.

"But God can see everything," most of them reply.

"God is a permissive God. He wants you to show Him the error of your ways, pray for a God-centered life, and live free of past and present transgressions. I repeat, 'God cannot heal what He cannot see.'"

We spot-check everything. We plunge deep into the deadly sins of pride, lust, covetousness, anger, gluttony, envy, and sloth. We continue a searching and fearless moral inventory and go after any traits of character that keep the aspirant sick.

Louella came to us following a messy, dirty-money divorce. A native Texan, Louella took her settlement and bought a large working ranch outside Dallas. She was determined to get on with her life, but her low self-esteem was camouflaged by fancy clothes, flashy jewelry, and a frenetic need to find a man.

"Louella, why don't you let me know who you really are? Write down what you like and dislike about yourself. List your assets and liabilities as you would for a bank," I told her.

The next day we got to the nitty-gritty. Louella had a strange list:

1. I know how to shop and dress well.

2. I have good taste in jewelry.

3. I am generous to people I like.

4. I paint well.

"Louella, may I reassess your value to yourself? Rather than focus on the outside, let's look at your internal reserves. How about your unwavering faith that God is in charge of your life and that He will put into your life what He wants you to have? That sure beats good-looking designer clothes, eh, kid?

"When you got divorced, you bought the ranch in your own name with your own credit and you made a decision to go to any lengths—against great odds—to make it successful. I'll take that over jewelry any day, won't you, Louella?"

When you inventory who you are and what you have to offer, examine what is of value to you. Do you put more stock in a big home, fancy car, expensive wardrobe, or posh restaurants than you do in how you feel about who and what you are? You are not your house not your car; you are a precious child of God who is on planet Earth to overcome transgressions past and present and to learn to be happy, joyous, and free every day that you live.

Go through your liabilities and name them one by one. Unattractive qualities are most often ones we develop to insulate ourselves against emotional hurt.

A typical homework assignment: "Write about gossip and whom you talk about. Gossip is a form of character assassination. We all do it to a lesser or greater degree. Gossip is always the communication of weak and insecure people.

"Make a list of all people about whom you gossip. Write down what you have said, your source material, and how this has been harmful to those on your list. Imagine that for every one person you gossip about, three people are talking about you. You get back what you give. If you refuse to talk about others, the rumors about you will cease. Try it. It never fails.

"When you hear biting and stinging gossip about yourself and the bearer of bad tidings says to you, 'And whatever you do, don't tell her that I told you,' say back, 'tell someone who cares.

The king always killed the messenger,' and then turn and walk away."

Barbara came kicking and screaming to Sedona for her week. Barbara was born in Georgia and raised in Tennessee. A former college beauty and runner-up Miss America in the mid-fifties, Barbara had gained a hundred pounds over thirty years and wore garish makeup and gaudy clothes and cursed like a sailor.

She was in a loveless marriage and had a hard time forgiving her husband of more than twenty years for an affair ten years earlier. She almost turned around and went home the minute she arrived in Sedona, because her husband was having a panic attack with her out of town. They never traveled without the other. Billy was missing Momma. This was the same husband she couldn't forgive for the old-flame affair. But she couldn't divorce him because "What would the neighbors think?" Southerners ... go figure.

After Barbara and I talked and meditated, she had a major shift in priorities and values. Here is the list of things she considered personal liabilities:

1. I talk about people behind their backs all the time. [Don't forget that gossip indicates a weak person with low self-esteem.]

2. I eat junk food and watch television when my husband thinks I am at the gym. [Food is an addiction, like booze and drugs. Barbara needed to see that she uses food to cover deeper and more painful issues.]

3. I always look at what's wrong with someone instead of seeing their good qualities. [This is low self-esteem again. Building ourselves up by tearing others down never works. Addictions drive us to make ourselves better at someone else's expense.]

Barbara finally got the program. She looked at the macabre world within and learned to love herself through the process of forgiveness and acceptance.

If you are overweight, something more dangerous than food lurks inside you. Overeating is a smoke screen for deeper issues. Psychiatrists and psychologists are finding that sexual abuse and incest trigger many eating disorders, including bulimia and anorexia. A deep and thorough inventory in all areas of your life will do more for you than all the antidepressants, exotic vacations, and golf games in the world.

All the reading and writing and journal-keeping and praying and meditating will not bring deep soul relief if you don't confess your shortcomings. You do that with me and the psychologist. Freedom from the bondage of self and others is what you will feel when you complete your Intensive.

Not all clients come looking for solutions to addiction to booze, drugs, food, or other destructive habits. Some come running for answers to a tragedy that blindsides them.

Katherine and Arthur lived in St. Louis with three children. Katherine was a pediatrician and Arthur a stockbroker. Their children were good students, athletic, and well behaved. Katherine and Arthur seemed the handsome couple with picture-perfect children. They were Catholics, members of the country club and everyone envied them for being the ideal American family. One day when Katherine and Arthur were away for the weekend their youngest child committed suicide. Family and friends asked over and over, "What made Laura kill herself?"

When they came to speak with me, I told Katherine and Arthur that I would work with them, but separately, and then we could commiserate in group when both finished their week.

From day one, I set one irrefutable ground rule: It would be understood that Laura had made a decision to end her own life. No matter what had or had not happened at home, no one but

Laura was responsible for her death. In helping someone work through the dark, hard spots of grief, it is important to free survivors from guilt and remorse. No one is culpable in a suicide but the one who kills himself.

What freed Katherine and Arthur most was recognizing how powerless they were over Laura's death. You can love and nurture, coddle and cuddle children and lovers as sentimental smother-mothers, and still not make them choose to live. They left Sedona determined to listen more carefully to their other two children and to encourage them to talk about anything bothering them, no matter how insignificant it seemed to be. Their primary responsibility was to love their children.

"I feel free of angst and remorse about Laura's suicide and connected in a liberated way to Polly and Ken, Laura's sister and brother. Getting them to have the courage to face their fears and the willingness to open up to us parents with whatever is bothering them is part of my responsibility as a parent," Arthur told me as we said our good-byes.

You are your brother's keeper.

When their time in Sedona comes to a close, there is one final bit of unfinished business that frees the participant from resentments and gnawing revenge: the client writes amends letters to all those people he has harmed. Whatever has been raging and eating at him, once the exercise with forgiveness letters has been completed, he leaves Sedona determined to live a life that no longer has him connected to remorse and regret. He is clear.

Forgiveness is the path to clearing.

Chapter 2

A Letter of Forgiveness

And forgive us our trespasses,
As we forgive those who trespass against us.
—*Book of Common Prayer,* Morning Prayer

Forgive: to cease to feel resentment against an offender; to make amends, to make things better
—*Webster's Ninth New Collegiate Dictionary*

Dear Dad:

I am in Sedona, Arizona, going through a powerful program of clearing. After a week of facing years of resentment, anger, and rage, I was asked to write a letter of forgiveness to anyone I had harmed in my life. After me, you were the first person I thought of. I needed to write you this letter.

The hook to a letter of forgiveness is that I must ask for your forgiveness rather than to expect you to seek my forgiveness. This was real hard at first, until I began to understand what forgiveness is.

When you and Mom divorced around my ninth birthday, I thought I had done something wrong. When money ran low and she had to work two jobs to support us kids, I thought it was my fault. When we heard that you lost your job of over twenty-five years, I wondered what I could have done to prevent that. In recovery I have focused less on what you did to harm me and more on how powerless I am to change anyone's life but my own. The thing I discovered about me is that I am selfish and self-centered. You did what you did because that's what you wanted to do. I have let your actions upset and enrage me for over thirty years.

Dad, the most amazing thing happened to me when I did an inventory about my childhood. I actually remembered some of the good times, which included you. Remember that summer you came to camp to see me and John and you brought him a kayak and me a bow and arrows? I became a marksman and took blue ribbons three years straight. John and I both laughed and kidded each other for years, because his kayak kept sinking while my arrows kept hitting the bull's-eye. I never told you how much I wanted to win because you had given me the bow and arrows. And the time you came to watch me play in the junior tennis finals and I got beat the first round, you were supportive of my abilities. The next year I won division singles title. I never thanked you for the bow and arrows and for the support with no criticism of my tennis ability.

During the process we have to write about the family, which includes background information on you and Mom. As I started to reconstruct your childhood, I found out by talking to Grandmother and Granddaddy that you had some difficult situations to work through. Grandmother said that you were born during the Depression and had to drop out of college in order to help the family with living expenses. She said that there were no student loans and that Granddaddy retired early at half-pension because of a disability. Money was tight, and it took you seven years to get your degree. You were an honors student and a top-flight debater. And you worked sixty hours a week for over four years.

Dad, that alone began to weaken my argument that you didn't understand me and how hard working and going to school was.

When I asked Grandmother why you never told me about all this when you and I would argue about my grades in college, she said, "That's just the way Jim is."

The more I heard about you, the more I began to relate to what you were doing and how you were feeling. Before, I looked at how you had harmed me by not being a part of our family. Now I see benefits to not having had you at home.

Every time I would hear about the "inner child" and how he affects everything I do, I wanted to throw up. But as I listened and became more honest, I realized that there was a hurt, sensitive little kid in me who was afraid of intimacy and of being harmed. You probably know that I have been married and divorced twice and have a daughter from one marriage and a son from another. I swore that I would never get divorced, and yet I did.

The more I reached inside to rescue my kid and help him get what he never got—love, companionship, nurturing, and acceptance—the less thin-skinned and touchy I became. And I don't see myself as a victim of a broken home; rather, that's the hand life dealt me.

I have been going to SLAA (Sex and Love Addicts Anonymous), a twelve-step program that is helping me learn how to have a loving relationship with another human being. It is amazing how fearful I was about my sexuality, until I took a thorough and fearless moral inventory of my actions. Hurting others was much higher on the list than what others did to me.

Dad, the bottom line is that I never called you or sent cards on Father's Day, your birthday, or Christmas. I never cared about your feelings, but only about poor little old me. That is going to change.

From this day forth, you will be my dad and I will love you without conditions. I will not speak of you with malice and disrespect, and I want only God's blessings for you, and for you to be happy, joyous, and free.

I want to ask you to forgive me for my shortcomings and how I have been hurtful to you. I want to make amends by changing how I perceive you and treat you. Dad, will you forgive me? By the way, the forgiveness deal says that your response to my forgiveness letter is none of my business. Writing the letter is all I am responsible for. I love you, Dad.

Alex

P.S. I would like for you to meet me at my old summer camp, Oak Mountain Fresh Air Farm, for the twenty-fifth reunion in August. I have entered us in the Father-Son Archery Contest.

When Alex finished his letter of forgiveness, he was in tears and needed reassurance that his emotions were legitimate. I told him that his true feelings were releasing him from self-imposed bondage and shame. Asking his dad's forgiveness opened Alex up to freedom for the first time in his life. The stuffed feelings about his father affected all the relationships in his life, particularly with wives and children. Resentments had kept him in a prison of emotional isolation.

"What do I do next?" he asked.

"You must burn your forgiveness letters. Ancient Indian rite of passage says that you must come to Mother and seek forgiveness. Mother is Mother Earth. You must go out into the Red Rocks and find a place that calls you. You must sit and meditate, then read your letters aloud to the Mother Earth spirit. When your soul has been prepared for the power and magic of ceremony, you must burn and bury your letters of forgiveness."

In addition to the letter of forgiveness to his father, Alex had to write letters to his mother, two ex-wives, two children, three siblings, and several former employers. The letters of forgiveness must include anyone toward whom deep and toxic resentments have festered harmful attitudes and inappropriate actions.

The effectiveness of amends letters is enhanced by the anger and rage letters that Alex and other clients write. Anger and rage bring all shame, hurt, revenge, disappointment, and hidden fears topside, where mental health can infuse wellness. It is always what one cannot access and express that makes one the sickest longest.

Getting to the natural progression of clearing requires taking every step toward freedom from bondage of self and others. In laying his family history on the table, slipping in God consciousness as a sidebar, and then taking his sexual inventory, the client makes significant passage in coming out of hiding and taking off ridiculous masks. Assets and liabilities and harm done and perpetrated finish the litany of what blocks the sunshine of the spirit and how the ego snaps up another victim. Quite simply, each client finds out that he learned everything he knew from parents, teachers, preachers, and peers who didn't have a clue about who they were and how to get home to God. "Monkey see, monkey do" paralyzed all of us into becoming the same defective prototype of poorly put-together humanity.

Each client is given directions on how to prepare the Earth to receive all his hurt and pain and letters of release. First Alex started the rite of passage by becoming tomb-still. He cleared his mind of chatter and clutter. Alex brought my meditation tape and a Walkman so he would have an audible companion as he began the final journey from darkness into light—from confusion to clearing.

When he sensed that he had prepared himself to offer up his forgiveness letters to the Earth, he began to read aloud each letter. When finished, he clutched the letter to his heart and closed his eyes to allow Mother Earth time to receive his plea for forgiveness. Then he dug a small hole, struck a match, and burned the letter to ashes in its grave. After the letter had burned, he covered the ashes with dirt and placed a stick perpendicular to the ground, with three small rocks as a marker for the forgiveness-letter grave. Each forgiveness letter has its own sepulcher, and they are dug in a semicircle.

Alex repeated this process for every letter, pausing between each burning to show Mother Earth proper respect and to allow the transference in the universe from transgression to forgiveness. When all letters had been burned, he dug a pit and burned the week's worth of inventory without reading it. The inventory ashes he marked with a large stick and three bigger rocks.

The graves for the forgiveness letters and the pit of ashes for the week's homework form the eye of Horus from Egyptian mythology. Horus symbolizes death and resurrection. The letter-burning ceremony links the ritualistic traditions of the Native American Indian with an Egyptian rite. Many believe that northern Arizona, including Sedona, was colonized by migrants from the land of the Nile.

When he finished his ceremony of surrender through amends and forgiveness, Alex tore out of his private burial ground and sanctuary with whoops of joy. He ran up to Scott and me and gave us both tight bear hugs. "I love you, Scott. I love you, Albert. I love life and I'm free!"

Love is all there is.

Alex felt the way all the seekers and searchers feel. Each comes to Sedona prepared for the battle royal, determined to hang on to resentments and splices of film from childhood that nothing would make them give up. And each one does give them up, in his time and in his own way. Inventory plus the magic of Red Rock Country stare the impish and destructive ego in the face, and the ego loses every time. God prevails by the power of truth, love, and beauty, in the name of peace, balance, and harmony.

"Albert, I want to thank God and you and all the therapists and the vortices—and me for having the courage to go through this clearing. I've been a scrapper, a bulldog competitor, and a cavalier Casanova, but I have never felt as connected to who I really am in my entire life. I have no more regrets, and there is nothing else I feel compelled to do to make me feel better about me. If I die in the next five minutes, I will fly into eternity as free as a bird." Alex hugged me tightly and sobbed himself into release from the bondage of self and others. I rocked him back and forth as Mother Earth whispered for me to do.

Alex went home and practiced what he had learned in Sedona. He stayed straight and sober, and his life changed completely. Every day was a challenge, but he was able to meet it head-on and as whom he really is.

It is my hope that you will experience the great awakening in your life that I did in mine and that the eight life lessons that were given to me may be of benefit to you. I would encourage you to seek divine guidance from your High Self as I did with mine. Do not be discouraged when you intuitively call the name of your spiritual guide and he does not answer on the first or second try. Be patient and ask often for help with your life's purpose. There are no calendars or clocks to announce when that moment of deep and abiding connection to a power greater than yourself will click connect for you. This is the promise: God will speak to you when you pray and you will hear his answers if you listen.

May God bless you and keep you as you interconnect and interrelate to all your brothers and sisters along your spiritual path.

ACKNOWLEDGMENTS

I will always be eternally grateful to Chris Anderson. Your constant care and concern to make sure that all elements of the book were completed in a timely fashion were invaluable.

I owe heartfelt thanks to editor Laurie Masters of Precision Revision. You did a superb job to reshape the book to make it read more smoothly.

Steve Hansen, I will be forever in your debt for creating a beautiful dust cover and masterfully designing the book itself.

I want to thank you, Gail, David, Ashley and Andrew Bell, for your friendship and encouragement; you are First Family for me.

God got Sagan Lewis to urge me to write a book. For your insistence and encouragement I will be eternally grateful.

To consciousness-raising James and Salle Merrill-Redfield, there are not enough words to express my thanks to you both for all the years of friendship and support of me and Scott and the work we do.

My heartfealt thanks to Shawn Stryker for all of her assistance and only she knows how important she has been to this project.

I acknowledge and thank my dear friends and support team from Birmingham: Cathy Ovson Friedman, my closest friend and confidante, and her husband, Paul "make me laugh" Friedman; Louise Nagrodzki Abroms, my heart and soul; Kathy G. Mezrano, live wire and eternally supportive friend and Frank Stitt, chef and owner of Birmingham's crown jewel, the Highlands Bar & Grill, who always reserves me the best table.

I will always appreciate and have deep and abiding gratitude for you, Joann Davis, for all the years of genius help and friendship.

My lifelong love and thanks go out to the No. 1 angel of us all, Larry Kirshbaum.

For your spiritual guidance and friendship, I want to thank my soul sisters, the nuns at the Sarada Convent in Santa Barbara, California.

And foremost to my spiritual teacher, Swami Swahananda of the Vedanta Society of Southern California: I am humbled by your willingness to be a part of this book and grateful for you steering me in the right direction when I lost my way.

I want to thank my brothers and sisters, Mary, Bill, Henry, Jeannie, and Margie, and especially my parents, for making me be true to myself.

And to my dear, dear Southern friend, Jim Bob Winfrey I thank a million times over for believing in me and my work. You have known me before and after my bout with alcoholism and you have remained one of my closest allies. Your love and support mean the world to me.

Always I am thankful for the Sedona Intensive support team, Rich Schonberg and Jean Neesley; Mountain Dove Chiropractic practitioners, Marc and Jan Viafora, and office manager, Taranga; Phil Wharton of Wharton Performance; Prasado Kendzia, Katherine LaToracca, Garielle Drumm, and Kedzi Morgan. Without you there would be no Sedona Intensive.

I want to acknowledge my Saturday-morning sober group for keeping me sane and sober. You are my lifeline.

And to every single client who ever went through the Sedona Intensive, I thank you for my clearing.

I want to give my heartfelt thanks to Dorothy Wood Espiau for being such a good friend and a positive force in my life. More than anything you have taught me that when I think I am down and out, it's not the real me. Authentic Albert, according to you, is always ready to finish the assignment I accepted this lifetime.

Dorothy, I will always love you and be eternally grateful to you for making such a difference in my life. Check it!

I will always be indebted to Beirne Waters Richmond for all the love and support you have given me for more than twenty-five years. When I did not think I could persevere, you held out a hand, and when I needed assistance you never gave me a stone. I will always love you, and I send God's blessings to you every single day, dear friend.

I want to thank Susie Barker Lavenson for all the help she offered for fun and for free to this project. Susie, when you and Jim Lavenson restored the San Ysidro Ranch in 1973, I was able to write books and a movie there and simply luxuriate in the beauty and serenity of the Montecito mountaintop. The cottages were furnished with country French appointments and very cozy—my home away from home. It was truly Paradise on Earth during the Lavenson years.

I would be remiss if I forgot darling Leonora Hornblow, my muse and dearest friend for more than twenty years. You are gone but not forgotten by me. Who I have become I attribute to your wise counsel. From the bottom of my heart I love you and miss you every single day.

I owe a debt of gratitude to Susan Sarandon, because you are the bravest person I know—you speak your truth and stand in harm's way so that all of us may live in a freer world. When your eyes widen and you open your mouth to speak unrehearsed, I look and I listen, and oftentimes walk to the beat of your drummer. You are kind and you are gentle. Your humility convicts me when mine goes missing. I am a better person for having known you.

I thank you, Paulo Coelho, and your tuning fork a million times over for awakening all of us who are warriors of the light to our mission in the world. God bless you and your masterpiece, *The Alchemist*, which helped me discover the Santiago within me.

ECLIPSES

2006
9/7 lunar eclipse: 15 degrees of Pisces
9/22 solar eclipse: 29 degrees of Virgo

2007
3/3 lunar eclipse: 12 degrees of Virgo
3/19 solar eclipse: 28 degrees of Pisces
8/12 solar eclipse: 19 degrees of Leo
8/28 lunar eclipse: 4 degrees of Pisces

2008
2/7 solar eclipse: 17 degrees of Aquarius
2/21 lunar eclipse: 1 degrees of Virgo
8/1 solar eclipse: 9 degrees of Leo
8/16 lunar eclipse: 24 degrees of Aquarius

2009
2/9 lunar eclipse: 20 degrees of Leo
2/15 solar eclipse: 6 degrees of Pisces
7/7 lunar eclipse: 15 degrees of Capricorn
7/22 solar eclipse: 29 degrees of Cancer
8/6 lunar eclipse: 13 degrees of Aquarius
8/20 solar eclipse: 27 degrees of Leo
12/16 lunar eclipse: 24 degrees of Sagittarius
12/31 solar eclipse: 10 degrees of Cancer

2010
6/12 solar eclipse: 21 degrees of Gemini
6/26 lunar eclipse: 4 degrees of Capricorn
12/5 solar eclipse: 13 degrees of Sagittarius
12/21 lunar eclipse: 29 degrees of Gemini

2011
6/1 solar eclipse: 11 degrees of Gemini
6/15 lunar eclipse: 24 degrees of Sagittarius
12/10 lunar eclipse: 18 degrees of Gemini
12/14 solar eclipse: 2 degrees of Capricorn

2012
6/4 lunar eclipse: 14 degrees of Sagittarius
6/19 solar eclipse: 28 degrees of Gemini
11/13 solar eclipse: 21 degrees of Scorpio
11/28 lunar eclipse: 6 degrees of Gemini

Bibliography

Arguelles, Jose. *The Mayan Factor*. Rochester, VT: Bear, 1987.

Bobrick, Benson. *The Fated Sky: Astrology in History*. New York: Simon & Schuster, 2005.

Brown, Lester. *Plan B 2.0: Rescuing a Planet Under Stress and a Civilization in Trouble*. New York: W. W. Norton, 2006.

Calleman, Carl Johan. *Solving the Greatest Mystery of Our Time : The Mayan Calendar*. Coral Springs, FL: Garev, 2000.

Calleman, Carl Johan. *The Mayan Calendar and the Transformation of Consciousness*. Rochester, VT: Bear, 2004.

Campbell, Joseph with Bill Moyers. *The Power of Myth*. New York: Anchor, 1991.

Carreon, Hector. *Apocalypto: Gibson's next film and the Mayan year 2012*. La Voz de Aztlan. http://www.aztlan.net/apocalypto.htm. August 22, 2005.

Cerminara, Gina. *Many Mansions*. Salem, OR: Signet, 1988.

Coelho, Paulo. *The Alchemist*. San Fransisco: Harper, 1993.

Conway, Flo and Jim Sigelman. *Snapping: America's Epidemic of Sudden Personality Change*. New York: Stillpoint Press, 1978

Davis, Ken. *Don't Know Much About Mythology*. New York: Harper Collins, 2005.

Easwaran, Eknath. *The End of Sorrow: The Bhagavad Gita for Living, Vol. 1*. Tomales, CA: Nilgiri, 1979.

Emoto, Masaru. *The Hidden Messages in Water*. New York: Atria, 2004.

Fiore, Edith. *Encounters: A Psychologist Reveals Case Studies of Abductions by Extraterrestrials*. New York: Ballantine, 1989.

Fiore, Edith. *The Unquiet Dead*. New York: Ballantine, 1987.

Flanangan, G. Patrick. *Pyramid Power: The Millenium Science*. Anchorage, AK: Earthpulse, 1997.

Gaulden, Albert Clayton. *Signs and Wonders: Understanding the Language of God*. New York: Atria, 2003.

Gaulden, Marguerite Fissell. *Poems that My Mother Wrote*. Sedona, AZ: Sedona Intensive, 1992.

Gibbon, Edward. *The Decline and Fall of the Roman Empire*. New York: Alfred A. Knopf, 1993.

Greeson, Judith. *It's Not What You're Eating, It's What's Eating You*. New York: Pocket, 1994.

Hall, Manley. *The Secret Teachings of All Ages*. New York: Tarcher/Penguin, 1984.

Harris, Sam. *The End of Faith: Religion, Terror and the Future of Reason*. New York: W.W. Norton, 2004.

Jung, C.G. *Synchronicity: An Acasual Connecting Principle*. New Jersey: Princeton, NJ: University Press, 1960.

Kasser, Rodolphe, Marvin Meyer, and Gregor Wurst, ed. *The Gospel of Judas*. Washington, DC: National Geographic, 2006.

Khayyam, Omar. *Rubaiyat of Omar Khayyam*. Whitefish, MT: Kessinger, 2003.

Kubler-Ross, Elisabeth. *On Death and Dying: What the dying have to teach doctors, nurses, clergy and their own families*. New York: Scribner, 1997

M. *The Gospel of Sri Ramakrishna*. New York: Ramakrishna-Vivekananda Center, 1942.

MacLaine, Shirley. *The Camino: A Journey of the Spirit*. New York: Atria, 2001.

MacLaine, Shirley. *Out on a Limb*. New York: Bantam, 1986.

King James Bible. Nashville, TN: Thomas Nelson, 1990.

Peck, M. Scott. *People of the Lie: The Hope for Healing Human Evil*. New York: Touchstone, 1983.

Prabhavananda, Swami and Christopher Isherwood. *How to Know God: The Yoga Aphorisms of Pantanjali*. New York: Ramakrishna-Vivekananda Center, 1996.

Redfield, James. *The Celestine Prophecy*. New York: Warner, 1993.

Robinson, James M., ed. *The Nag Hammadi Library: The Definitive Translation of the Gnostic Scriptures Complete in One Volume*. San Francisco: Harper, 1990.

Sadat, Jehan. *A Woman of Egypt*. New York: Simon & Schuster, 1987

Sanford, John. *The Invisible Partners: How the Male and Female in Each of Us Affects Our Relationships*. New York: Paulist Press, 1980.

Shakespeare, William. *As You Like It*. 1599.

Sierra, Javier. *The Secret Supper*. New York: Atria, 2004.

Stevenson, Robert Louis. *A Child's Garden of Verses*. New York: Simon & Schuster, 1999.

Tarnas, Richard. *Cosmos and Psyche: Intimations of a New World View*. New York: The Penguin Group, 2006.

Wise, Michael O., Martin Abegg, Jr., and Edward Cook. *The Dead Sea Scrolls: A New Translation, Translation and Commentary*. San Francisco: HarperSanFrancisco, 1999.

About the Front Cover:

Mexican-born Artist Octavio Ocampo was educated at the Fine Art Institute, Mexico City and the San Francisco Art Institute, graduating in 1974.

His works are in major collections in Mexico, the National Palace, and the collections of the last three presidents. The King of Spain is also a great admirer. Ocampo is the master of his métier and unique among today's painters.

Celebrity portraits for which Ocampo has been commissioned in the United States include President Jimmy Carter (commissioned by President Lopez Portillo and presented as a gift from the United Mexican States), Jane Fonda, Cher (for the front and back covers of one of her albums), and César Chávez.

Ocampo now works and resides in Tepoztlan, north of Mexico City, considered to be one of the most magical places on Earth.

He works primarily in the metamorphic style—using a technique of superimposing and juxtaposing realistic and figurative details within the images that he creates.

If you are interested in purchasing a gicleé print of "Buddha," the image on the front cover, please visit:

www.artistspublishing.com.

SEDONA INTENSIVE AVAILABLE

Go through the Sedona Intensive with Albert Gaulden and Scott Carney and their amazing team of therapists and practitioners. Experience a deep, enduring soulful healing in the magical Red Rock Country. Face your fears—tear down ego blocks—that have kept you from a happy, joyous, and free life. Discover the real you with certified counselors, professional therapists, personal fitness trainers, network chiropractors, a voice coach, and pampering massages, yoga, sunset hikes, and much more.

To receive a brochure or for further information, write:

The Sedona Intensive

P.O. Box 2309

Sedona, AZ 86339-2309

or call (928) 282-4723

Private astro-intuitive telephone sessions are available.
Please inquire.

Our website is:

www.sedonaintensive.com.

An Interview with the Author

Q: How did you happen to write this book?

A. I work with a lot of people who say that there are two or more people living inside of them and they didn't know which one they were. They asked constantly, "Who am I?" "I can't be someone who would be unfaithful to his wife, drink like a fish and purport to be one way and act another." In my work as an astro-intuitive therapist I help the client uncover the authentic self by exposing all the imposters who try to live inside his head. My therapists and I have to get the client to look at compulsions and addictions, and I am not talking exclusively about drugs and alcohol. Greed and corporate malfeasance, lying and manipulation from government, physical abuse, sexual problems and split personalities are proliferating on a par with global warming. These areas people need to clear up and they do with our Intensive. Since I am a transpersonal counselor and am not held to the same standards as a psychologist, I tell my story to clients and in this book, including my recovery from alcoholism and other compulsions. A lot of people asked me to write how I came to be authentic, so here is how I did become the real Albert.

Q. You are very out front about your lack of trust in traditional religion. How do you grow up a Baptist and then with booze as an *aide-de-camp* throw out your faith?

A. Let me be clear about one thing: my faith is stronger than it ever has been. I think that I became aware that what I was being taught as a child and then as an adult was not true for me. There is an intriguing book, *Snapping: America's Epidemic of Sudden Personality Change* by Flo Conway and Jim Siegelman that talks about how one comes out from under the suppressive control of a religion or cult. Using their language I think I snapped out of Baptist mind control. Conditioning does not go away in a nanosecond.

Awareness comes after a lot of pain and soul-searching. But I think this is where reincarnation comes into play. Somewhere in my past lives, I had been the authoritarian religious leader who controlled followers, and now I have had the experience of clearing away the distortion and lies of my past and present lives, and I am on assignment to help other people find their true God—the one within themselves.

Q. I find the concept of a High Self within each of us fascinating. Can you be more specific exactly how you communicate with your High Self, Paul?

A. In the beginning stages of my contact with Paul, I was in a deep meditation. I intuited through thought impressions what he wanted to tell me. With the passage of time, I began to speak and write and teach as my Albert self, although his influence is always with me. But I no longer need to be in meditation to receive his words and thoughts. As distinct as I explain this relationship, a lot of people who want either to channel displaced persons or the unquiet dead or get messages through a medium from them, cannot wrap their minds around who Paul is and how we work together. All my work with him is mind-to-mind and through intuition. I wrote his side of the conversation because this was the information his thoughts were helping me to remember.

Q. Remembering is an interesting subject. You write that we remember, we don't learn anything new. Can you expand on that?

A. Remembering predisposes us to accepting the notion of reincarnation. If we live life after life, and if the same soul lives on, it would follow that we have a memory bank of what we've ever done or been to draw from. Since everything has been in master consciousness since the beginning of time, all knowledge is available to us. The trick is to break the illusion of ego limitation. Ego tries to tell us that God and the always-was-and-always-is-world is a lot of hooey. Ego is the great deceiver and should be embraced and reeducated.

Q. Lesson 2, **God or No God?** may differ with a lot of people's religious dogma. What happened to heaven and God on a throne?

A. I wrote the lesson as I did to tease atheists and agnostics. Nietzsche said, "God is dead." I say he is very alive and living inside each of us. I find it amazing that the United States was founded on religious freedom and yet religions in this country, particularly when influenced by the political right, have far too much control over the lives of Christians. We patriots need to wake up and find our own God and read our own insightful scriptures and self-legislate how we will pray. True religious freedom is a birthright.

Q. You call yourself an ordinary man but you write about some famous people, like Shirley MacLaine and Madame Sadat. How do you meet these people and the rest of us are stuck in the neighborhood of familiarity and ordinary?

A. It is the law of attraction. Each of us draws people and situations to us like metal to a magnet. Some people come into our lives to bless us and others to cause us trouble. I attract famous people, perhaps, to remind me that being an ordinary man living an extraordinary life is better than fame. Although some find the concept of reincarnation a bit nutty, I know we live life after life after life. Perhaps, I have known these people in another life; perhaps we met again for an energy exchange, to activate a memory or to give each other a piece of the puzzle we need to solve our riddle.

John Travolta fell over my foot in a restaurant and I sold him a 35-acre land grant estate above Santa Barbara. I wasn't born to sell real estate. How did I do it? That story is a book unto itself. Why me? Why not me? Wouldn't it be interesting if this land had been his in a former life and I had stolen his birthright? "Let's pretend" helps us decipher who did what to whom, when, and why we meet again.

Q. How can an ordinary person develop his intuition?

A. Learning to meditate daily is the best tool I can offer. Silence is where intuition speaks. Keeping a journal removes clutter from the head and puts it on the journal pages. This frees up the mind to receive thought impressions. Join a reputable self-awareness class. I suggest that someone who wants to turn up the volume of his still small voice of intuition put in the time—go to class week after week and one day he will hear the voice and receive the direction he is looking for. When you develop your own intuition you will know what is true for you and you will stick with it, no matter what you read or hear from anyone else.

Q. Lessons 3 is **The Light Will Never Fail**. How do you explain evil? What is required to enlighten one's dark side?

A. Living in the light and staying stuck on the dark side is an interesting proposition. Dr. Scott Peck, who wrote *People of the Lie* said that when you encounter evil, which is the underpinning of narcissism, you must name it. Evil must be outed. A person who is evil can be redeemed if a concerned person is courageous enough to confront him about his dark side. Some of us laugh at exorcism, but an evil person needs more than ordinary therapy. Proceed cautiously when trying to dispel evil.

Dr. Scott Peck also points out that people become evil because they are constitutionally incapable of looking at themselves honestly. Honesty is as odious to an evil person as the name of God is to the ego.

Q. Discuss more about the shadow, or invisible partner, that makes relationships impossible.

A. None of us is taught or mentored about what relationships are all about and we certainly never heard that we had a shadow self. There is profound ignorance in why we can't make a partner out of our invisible partner, or shadow. We must see and hear our invisible partner; we must bond with the shadow, have a relationship with that part of ourselves. The difficulty is that men and women are at war, except the battlefield is at home. The war is over masculine dominance and female receptivity. Globally more people are alerted to the need to get to know their shadow selves, as well as to love themselves.

Q. You stress the importance of having our charts done to get to know ourselves better. Where do we find someone credible to do our chart?

A. You can call the American Federation of Astrologers at (480) 838-1751 or e-mail AFA@msn.com. We have two professional astro-intuitives on our staff. A birth chart, professionally prepared and read for you will give you truer knowledge of who you are than any other system I have ever used.

Q. You write about forgiveness. What if there is someone in your life you can't forgive. What do you do?

A. You stay stuck or move forward. Being unable to forgive someone lets me know you can't forgive yourself. The capacity to forgive is a huge piece of being able to become authentic. Remember that someone whom you can't forgive is not who you think he is or who he thinks he is either. When he clears, you both might be able to reconcile. Do your part now. Forgive and move on. Make no mistake: forgiving someone does not insinuate that you approve of his bad behavior.

We use Mountain Dove Chiropractic Clinic therapists in the Sedona Intensive. Here is how they describe how their patients find the ability to forgive.

"The body is greater than the sum of its parts. Our nervous system expresses an innate or resident intelligence which animates, motivates, heals, coordinates and inspires living beings. Health comes from the inside-out. By removing interference in the nervous system, our innate intelligence may better maintain each of our body's cells naturally."

Drs. Jan and Marc Viafora tell this story from their patient case studies: "As the nervous system heals, lives heal. Symptoms are there to get you to face yourself in the mirror. One woman cried and shook on the chiropractic adjusting table as she cleared an abuse situation involving her father that occurred fifty years ago. She told us that she realized forgiveness is more powerful than grief, hate and resentment." Amen.

Q. What is the one thing you want people to get from having read your book?

A. I want readers to know that no matter how painful is the process, heal all addictions and compulsions. Get well. Begin a search for the real self. If you have to tear your world apart like I did, so be it. Do not live the life anyone tells you to live except you, guided by your High Self, the God within you. Learn to speak the language of love and acceptance. And do not stop one minute before the miracle.

Other Works by Albert Clayton Gaulden

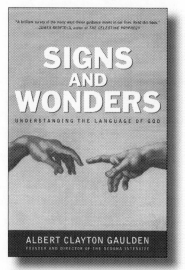

Hardcover: ISBN 0-734-4642-9   Paperback: ISBN 0-7432-3793-5

SIGNS AND WONDERS arrives at a perfect time when so many are looking for spiritual renewal in a world that is plagued by worry, doubt, and uncertainty. Gaulden has written a book that unveils the language of signs and wonders—its structure, vocabulary, syntax and grammar. He teaches us to be aware of the coincidences that happen to us all, and how to listen for the New Language—what he calls "God's mother tongue."

Major Endorsements

"A brilliant survey of the many ways divine guidance moves in our lives. Read this book."
— James Redfield, author of *The Celestine Prophecy*

"Discovering what is beyond discussion; talking about a language that is beyond words, this is our current task in order to create a dialogue among the warriors of the light. This book, **SIGNS AND WONDERS**, is an important step towards a new consciousness that will change the world."
— Paulo Coelho, author of *The Alchemist*

Order at www.sedonaintensive.com or call (800) 647-0732

Albert Gaulden's journey began when he received a remarkable message from his High Self and guide, Paul. It was at once an inspired vision of man's return to paradise during this new millennium and also a knowing mandate that he was to uncover his inner self and to pass that awareness on to other lost souls. This book reveals the mandate and how to discover one's own inner assignment.

Hardcover: ISBN 0-446-52019-5

A Clear Meditation for your Higher Self

Discover the Power Within

Albert wrote and recorded these meditations specifically to help you retrieve your authentic self. These are the meditation CD's that connect you to your High Self and bring you together with the greatest partnership you will ever have—a relationship with yourself.

Order at www.sedonaintensive.com or call (800) 647-0732